Knowledge-Based
Vision-Guided Robots

Studies in Fuzziness and Soft Computing

Editor-in-chief
Prof. Janusz Kacprzyk
Systems Research Institute
Polish Academy of Sciences
ul. Newelska 6
01-447 Warsaw, Poland
E-mail: kacprzyk@ibspan.waw.pl
http://www.springer.de/cgi-bin/search_book.pl?series=2941

Nick Barnes
Zhi-Qiang Liu

Knowledge-Based
Vision-Guided Robots

With 99 Figures
and 3 Tables

Physica-Verlag

A Springer-Verlag Company

Dr. Nick Barnes
University of Melbourne
Department of Computer Science
and Software Engineering
3010 Victoria
Australia
nmb@cs.mu.oz.au

Professor Zhi-Qiang Liu
City University of Hong-Kong
School of Creative Media
Tat Chee Ave., Kowloon
Hong Kong
P. R. China
zliu@cs.mu.oz.au

ISSN 1434-9922
ISBN 3-7908-1494-6 Physica-Verlag Heidelberg New York

Library of Congress Cataloging-in-Publication Data applied for
Die Deutsche Bibliothek – CIP-Einheitsaufnahme
Barnes, Nick: Knowledge based vision guided robots: with 3 tables / Nick Barnes; Zhi-Qiang Liu. – Heidelberg; New York: Physica-Verl., 2002
    (Studies in fuzziness and soft computing; Vol. 103)
    ISBN 3-7908-1494-6

Physica-Verlag Heidelberg New York
a member of BertelsmannSpringer Science+Business Media GmbH

© Physica-Verlag Heidelberg 2002
Printed in Germany

Hardcover Design: Erich Kirchner, Heidelberg

SPIN 10876877   88/2202-5 4 3 2 1 0 – Printed on acid-free paper

Acknowledgements

The authors would like to thank members of technical services of the department, particularly, John Horvath, Andrew Peel, Thomas Weichert, and David Hornsby, for keeping robots and cameras going, despite our best efforts to burn, crash, and destroy them in anyway possible.

Nick Barnes would also like to thank Andrew Howard, Sandy Dance, and Les Kitchen for the challenging research discussions. Thank-you to my family, Betty, Barry, Lisa and Dale for supporting me in this strange enterprise called research. Also, my other family John and Wendy for support, encouragement and Sunday dinners. Finally to Nina, the greatest person whom I know. Her inspiration is a great source of strength to me. Her support of everything that I do makes challenges seem easy. Her company makes problems seem trivial. Her smile makes everything else seem unimportant. Her writing and editing skills have improved this book beyond recognition. Without her help this book would never be completed.

*. . . if there were machines which bore a resemblance to
our body and imitated our actions as far as it was morally
possible to do so, we should always have two very certain
tests by which to recognise that, for all that, they were not
real men.*
R. Descarte. circa 1628. [95][1]

*I possessed the capacity of bestowing animation, yet to pre-
pare a frame for the reception of it, with all its intricacies
of fibres, muscles, and veins, still remained a work of in-
conceivable difficulty and labour.*
Frankenstein. Mary Shelley, 1818. [201]

*. . . to manufacture artificial workers is the same thing as
to manufacture motors. The process must be of the simplest,
and the product of the best from a practical point of view.*
R. U. R. (Rossum's Universal Robots). (English translation) Karel Capek, 1923. [39]

---

[1]See conclusion full text.

Contents

Chapter 1

Introduction

Robots have been a subject of philosophical inquiry and a source of literary inspiration for hundreds of years. It is only since this century that robots have emerged out of fiction and philosophy into the real world. Today robots are common-place, for instance, fixed-location robotic arms now tirelessly perform precise repetitive tasks for industry. However, robots still have significant limitations. Specifically, most industrial robots require the parts they operate on to be precisely aligned, and mobile robots that move around in an environment are still largely confined to academic research laboratories. Clearly, there is a need for a more advanced generation of robots that can react to unexpected events, and can complete complex tasks under less controlled conditions. To facilitate the advancement, systems must be developed that enable robots to perceive and understand their environment.

Perhaps the greatest potential benefit to humanity that robots can provide is to alleviate the need for humans to regularly perform tasks in dangerous environments, such as underground mines, underwater, in space, and in hazardous industrial environments. In such applications, robots can perform not only the tasks that humans currently undertake, but also handle operations that are too dangerous for individuals. The Soujourner Mars robot [158] gathered valuable information from the surface of Mars. This mission could not be carried out by humans as the craft was never to return to earth. As well, anti-personnel mines kill and maim civilians, but removing them is dangerous, hence robots could play an invaluable role in demining [168]. Finally, cleaning up in the aftermath of natural and human-made disasters (e.g., Chernobyl [159]) create highly dangerous environments for humans; these are environments where robots could excel.

In order to facilitate more advanced applications, robots need to be capable of more flexible autonomy than is currently possible. Robots need to be able to seek out and operate on target objects. This will enable tasks such as finding and removing dangerous objects (e.g., mines and nuclear material) returning to base stations and docking, and performing operations on objects that are dangerous for humans to access.

As a basis for such operations, robots require means for identifying and operating on specific objects. This book aims to take an initial step along this path, by constructing a framework to enable the robot to identify particular objects, when other similar objects may be present, and then navigate around the required objects. Importantly, the robot must have a knowledge of its approximate position with respect to the object. We call this task *circumnavigation*. This research is primarily concerned with autonomous robot navigation applications that require high-level perception to support their operation.

1.1   Background

Autonomous mobile robots are machines that are able to move around freely in a manner appropriate for their environment, with respect to some general goals. Control of the robot's movement in an environment is generally referred to as navigation. The earliest autonomous mobile robot was built by Dr. Grey Walter in the 1940's [230]. However, research in developing mobile robots as an end in itself began in earnest in the late 1960's with the development of vision-based robots such as 'Shakey' [169]. Recently, decreases in hardware costs have led to a flourish of research in robotics.

1.1.1   A vision-guided approach

Many types of sensors have been used by researchers as a basis for mobile robot perception. This book focuses almost exclusively on *vision-based sensors* that produce an image of light intensity values. Extensive discussion of other forms of sensors can be found in [75].

This book is directed at autonomous robot navigation applications that require high-level perception, for tasks such as uniquely identifying an object, when other similar objects are also visible. For such tasks, vision offers advantages in the type and amount of information it recovers in good lighting conditions. Sensors such as sonar are insensitive at a fine resolution, laser-range finders, and radar-like sensors can extract structural detail at a finer resolution, but cannot recover non-structural data, such as regions of different colour or reflective properties. Also, tactile sensors restrict operations by requiring physical contact.

1.1.2 Computer vision and vision-guided mobile robots

At present, research on *Computer Vision* and on *Vision-Guided Robot Navigation* forms an inadequate basis for the tasks required. When vision is used to guide robots, researchers often emphasise the use of techniques that are specialised to a particular application. Other more general vision techniques developed by the computer vision community, on the other hand, are too slow to be practically useful for mobile robot navigation.

Current research on vision guided-robotics often applies specific techniques for particular problems. For example, in road-following vehicles, systems such as that in [45] make assumptions [129] which are highly specific to road following. Some other mobile robot systems use only low-level features directly from the image, such as colour [196]. Little use has been made of high-level aspects of computer vision, such as three-dimensional (3D) object recognition, that are appropriate for large classes of problems and situations.

Computer vision methods are generally considered to be too cumbersome for real-world applications. This is a serious problem with most high-level techniques from traditional computer vision, where systems may often take minutes to complete processing a single image. This is clearly untenable for navigation where the robot has to move continuously. To maintain a speed of 10 cm/sec, a robot will often need to process a single image in a few seconds at most, and often multiple frames need to be processed per second. Slow processing may be acceptable only in exceptional circumstances.

Historically, most research in computer vision has been aimed at off-line systems, where an image is taken of an object or scene, from an unexpected, arbitrary angle that may be close to or far from the object. In particular, high-level vision often focuses mainly on the extraction of symbolic descriptions, and pays little attention to the speed of processing. The emphasis has been on exhaustive exploration of available image data. In many cases, researchers assume human intervention at stages that are impossible for an autonomous robotic system. For example, the shape-from-shading techniques assume that reflectance and lighting models are given, or that some of the surface normals are preset by manual intervention to offer boundary conditions [24].

1.1.3   Applying high-level computer vision to guide mobile robots

In order to apply high-level computer vision to robot navigation, methods that have fast response time, and can be used autonomously, are required. The methods must not rely on human intervention during operation. However, navigation does not require *general* computer vision. There are also additional constraints which follow from the fundamental differences between what is required in traditional computer vision, and what is required for robotic vision. Many differences follow from the fact that the camera is physically mounted on the robot, and the robot moves in a constrained way under its own control. This is referred to as *embodiment* [137]. Rather than having an isolated image from a random point in space, typically, a series of images are taken as the robot moves deliberately in continuous space. Systems utilising such differences need not be *ad-hoc*, but may be valid for a class of mobile robots.

This book aims to apply techniques from high-level vision for the purpose of mobile robot navigation. It is not adequate to take traditional high-level vision techniques and apply them to images from the camera of a mobile robot. Particular attention must be paid to reformulating the traditional vision methods to be appropriate for applications in mobile robot navigation. This book presents an operational robot system for navigating around objects. It also presents versions of high-level computer vision methods such as object recognition and shape-from-shading that have been designed specifically for robot navigation.

1.2   Aims of the Research Presented in this Book: A Problem in Robot Vision

The aim of this book is to develop computer vision methods that enable the robot to perform the following tasks:

1. The robot is required to be able to uniquely identify a single, specific known object placed randomly in an indoor environment

in which there may be other objects.

2. The robot must be able to move around the object maintaining a constant knowledge of its position relative to the object.

3. The robot is expected to be able to identify an object that cannot be uniquely distinguished from surrounding objects by simple features such as colour.

4. The robot is expected to be able to distinguish objects that have similar structure.

5. Edge-based matching of an object may not always be adequate; the robot must be able to distinguish objects based on surface shape.

6. The robot must be able to move around a corner of an object, so that all the object features that are initially visible become occluded, and new object surfaces are visible.

7. The robot cannot assume any prior knowledge of the object's position in the environment. It may not assume that it is facing any particular object surface. However, it may assume that the object is in the camera field of view.

8. The system should process each image of the scene within a few seconds, except in exceptional circumstances, such as recognising the object for the first time.

9. The system should be able to initially recognise the object from a large range of locations around it, although it is acceptable for the robot to misidentify based on a single view, as long this error is corrected once the robot has moved.

10. The robot is assumed to be ground-based, however, the methodology applied should not preclude extension into full 3D robot motion.

1.3   The Approach of this Book

In order to uniquely identify objects in the environment, it is necessary to compare robot sensor data to some form of object model. This book uses knowledge-based and model-based approaches to perception for mobile robots. The approach uses a model of required objects, and knowledge of the robot and camera, environment, and task required.

The system presented uses high order features, particularly edges and shapes, for object recognition. Such features are necessary to give the robot the discriminating power required. The approach here does not preclude supplementing these features with additional features such as colour and texture where necessary. However, these additional features are not used in the experiments in this book.

Vision is used primarily, as active sensors may not be adequate for distinguishing structurally similar objects. Also, to overcome the difficulties of discriminating objects with similar wire-frames, this book presents a method for verification of shape for candidate edge-based matches.

The proposed approach does not use methods of active vision, such as optical flow or visual servoing. Such methods are currently unable to handle occlusion of all visible surfaces. It is the author's belief that some form of model is required to allow the robot to recognise new surfaces that appear as part of the object.

Although, the approach assumes to know properties of the environment, it does not require a map of the environment in any form. Further, this book is concerned with the problems of navigation given an object model. It does not consider the problem of learning object models.

Finally, a vision-guided mobile robot must be able to translate perceptions to actions via motors. We examine the use of fuzzy control for this task.

1.4 About the Chapters

Chapter 2 describes a number of earlier vision-guided mobile robot systems and some concepts that are useful in a discussion of mobile robot navigation. This chapter focuses on vision-guided systems, rather than systems that employ active sensors (e.g., time-of-flight laser range finders, ultrasonic, radar, etc.), or use structured lighting (e.g., stripe-lasers). Also, the chapter presents aspects of computer vision research that are closely related to the approaches taken in this book.

Chapter 3 presents the philosophical basis of an approach to high-level computer vision for mobile robots, and a methodology for building systems of this nature. The development described in this book has been performed using this methodology.

Chapter 4 details an active object recognition system, which enables a mobile robot to recognise objects of arbitrary pose, and navigate safely around them. The chapter explicitly describes canonical-views and their use. It also presents a direct algebraic method for finding the pose and position of known objects in the camera's field of view.

Chapter 5 describes the methods for edge segmentation and matching that support the object recognition system in Chapter 4. These methods have been designed specifically for robot navigation guided by model-based computer vision.

Chapter 6 explores the derivation of shape from a single image to give greater certainty for object recognition than the edge-based approach described in Chapter 4. The research therein (i.e., a knowledge-based approach) is a new paradigm in early vision processing. The chapter demonstrates that the knowledge-based approach to shape-from-shading is able to solve problems that cannot be resolved by other methods. These problems arise in developing an object recognition system for an autonomous mobile robot. The approach is also able to find solutions faster than comparable methods in some cases.

Chapter 7 describes the methods used for navigation by the system including path planning, navigation, and obstacle avoidance methods employed to perform the tasks described in Chapter 4.

Chapter 8 presents a fuzzy control system for vision-guided reactive docking. It examines vision-guided mobile robot problems where fuzzy control is appropriate, and argues why fuzzy control is useful for these mobile robot control problems.

Chapter 9 presents the results of the system. The matching component is evaluated in isolation, and with the pose determination. The chapter then demonstrates the system in action through a number of case studies.

Chapter 10 concludes this book and highlights its contributions and its limitations. This chapter also suggests directions for future research on this topic.

Chapter 2

Related Systems and Ideas

Robot navigation has traditionally focussed on the problems of efficient, smooth, and effective motion in avoiding obstacles, and moving to a goal point. Frequently, perception is treated as something of a burden. Systems in the literature require some environmental information, and the perception used in those systems gives some noisy data about the environment. Many systems use active sensors such as laser range finders, which recover accurate structural data about the robot's surrounds. Such systems are efficacious on tasks that only require structural data, but are unable to handle situations that also require other data. This chapter is concerned specifically with vision-guided mobile robot navigation. Firstly, it presents some basic vision concepts and techniques to facilitate discussion of vision-guidance for mobile robots. Secondly, it presents basic concepts in robot navigation, and particularly vision-guided robot navigation, before describing some of the most effective for vision-guided robot navigation systems. Finally, this book is concerned with the application of high-level computer vision to robot navigation. Hence, the areas of computer vision that are relevant to this book are reviewed.

2.1 Basic computer vision approaches

We summarise a number of basic concepts and techniques in computer vision that the reader needs to be familiar with before we can present the ideas of vision-guided autonomous robots.

We wish to make a distinction, that is particularly relevant to vision-guided robot systems, between two general approaches to computer vision: frame-based, and image-sequence-based.

2.1.1   Frame-based computer vision

Until recently, the majority of vision-guided robot systems worked largely on the basis of single frames. The approach begins with early vision processing such as edge extraction, where neighbouring pixels with large differences in intensity are found, which often correspond to divisions between surfaces in front of the camera. The results of early vision processing are often formulated into a feature representation, such as segmented regions of the image. For robots such feature information is used to identify objects and locations, or determine robot pose relative to the environment, or some aspect of it. Frame-based approaches often work by extracting such information out of one image frame, and then planning and acting on the basis of this information. At some later stage another frame is taken and the process repeats.

Hough transform

The Hough transform is a commonly used method for finding straight-line edges, we use it here to exemplify the extraction of features following early vision processing. The Hough transform has also been extended for use extracting circles, ellipses, and corners. For straight edges, the basic idea is to re-parameterise edge pixels in line parameters. Any point can be described by the set of lines passing through it. Thus, for a set of colinear points there will be one line in common between all the points. The Hough method finds the set of lines for each point and then accumulates evidence to find straight-line segments. Different implementations have led to considerable computational savings in this scheme. For a full description, see [49].

2.1.2   Active vision

The other major approach is to use the changes between a sequence of images as the main source of data rather than the images themselves, this has also been called *motion analysis* [241]. This approach has seen only limited application in robotics although usage has increased in recent times. It is generally known as active vision. There are two general approaches within active vision which we distinguish, tracking and optical flow, although the boundaries are not entirely clear between them.

Tracking

Tracking follows the motion of a target as it moves through the camera's field of view. To do this requires solution of the temporal correspondence problem: matching the target in successive frames of a time sequence of images [92]. It is typical for the target to be either a set of features (e.g., edges), or an image region (e.g., a region of similar colour).

Optical Flow

Optical flow is the apparent motion in an image sequence, based on image differential measurements. It is related to the motion field, which is the two-dimensional projection of the three-dimensional motion of points relative to the camera [241]. However, problems such as scene lighting and surface reflection, and the aperture problem [241] combine to create differences between apparent motion and the motion field. These differences must be taken into account when using optical flow based measures for robot guidance.

The principle difference between optical flow and tracking based systems is that while tracking generally uses correspondence based on a target and finds the configuration and motion of the target, optical flow generally uses pixel-based properties such as differentials and finds a flow field for the whole image. Optical flow can be seen as pixel-based tracking, and tracking can be seen as feature-based optical flow.

2.2 Vision-Guided Mobile Robot Systems

The basic task of a mobile robot is to move through an environment to arrive at a destination point, possibly in a particular configuration. The configuration may consist only of a single orientation for a simple ground-based robot, or may be in many dimensions for an articulated robot, or a robot that moves in 3D (e.g., flying, underwater, or space robots). The destination may be: a position relative to the robot's initial starting point (e.g., move forward 1 metre); some spatial position with respect to a global coordinate system (e.g., meet me at my office); or may be a position relative to a particular feature, or set of features of the environment (e.g., move to the red car).

This section presents some basic functions required for robot navigation and the methods for performing them, along with some useful

concepts in mobile robot research. This section includes definitions of
these concepts for subsequent use in this book.

2.2.1 Mobile robot subsystems and concepts

In order to perform basic required tasks, a robot must have a means of
monitoring its position relative to goals. This book is interested in the
case when sensory perception is required, and a mechanical solution
(e.g., buried wires) will not suffice.

Dead-reckoning

Dead-reckoning tracks absolute robot position with respect to some coordinate frame by summing the accumulated robot motion. In wheeled
robots this is often achieved using odometry, where encoders monitor
wheel rotation (e.g., [165]). Interial data can also be used [14], and is a
standard form of dead-reckoning information when wheels are not used,
such as in underwater robots [114]. However, as dead-reckoning estimates drift over time and become increasingly poor [43], robot position
is often tracked by a combination of dead-reckoning and by recognising
some features in the world.

Global positioning system (GPS) is a satellite-based radio navigation system that can self-locate to within 5m anywhere on the globe
[14]. However, GPS can only be used outdoors, and other sensors are
required for more accurate positioning, also it has been criticised for
poor reliability [66].

Localisation

It is necessary for a robot to self-locate in some way with respect to
global coordinates for it to move around purposefully in a large environment, this is known as localisation.[1] This is generally performed by
recognising some feature or group of features (often called landmarks)
in the environment. The system may then have a position attached to
each landmark (in metric coordinates, or in terms of the environment
topology) which is used for path planning. Alternatively, it may have
navigation actions directly associated with landmarks, and thus only
implicit position (e.g., [111]).

---

[1]The degree of accuracy of localisation varies for different systems and applications. Some outdoor systems may only require a position estimate to within tens of
metres, whereas other indoor systems may be accurate to within centimetres.

Typically, robots localise periodically, and move by dead-reckoning in between localisations. Fusing localisation and dead-reckoning information often provides more accuracy for relative locations within a small area. Further, constantly localising is often infeasible: there may be a restricted range of locations where the robot can localise, or the cost of localisation may be expensive (e.g., an underwater robot that must surface in order to localise).

Localisation consists of two sub-problems of differing complexity. Firstly, the *drop-off* problem [215] is where the robot has no *apriori* knowledge of its position and so must consider all possible positions. Also, the *update* problem is where the robot has an estimate from a recent position, adding constraints to the possibilities of the current location.

Localisation methods can be separated approximately into two categories: those that modify the environment, such as adding some form of beacon (e.g., bar codes) [66, 119]; and, those that make use of items that typically appear in the robot's application environment [43]. The items are often particular to the environment of the robot application. Some research has been performed on selecting good natural landmarks from the environment [58, 240]. Methods that do not require environmental modification are generally far more demanding in terms of perception, but it is frequently infeasible to add beacons to the environment.

To illustrate natural landmark-based localisation, we present examples of both outdoor and indoor localisation systems. The systems take advantage of features that are particular to the required environments for localisation of a ground-based mobile robot. The first system (Talluri and Aggarwal [215]) operates in outdoor urban landscapes, localisation is performed by matching straight lines in the environment to a model[2] for a restricted subset of straight-line features of the environment, specifically roof-top edges. In the model, free-space in the environment is partitioned into non-overlapping regions over which the visibility list of edges is the same. As with many localisation-based systems, the search space is restricted using an approximate estimate of pose for the update problem. Talluri and Aggarwal also produced a system for mountainous regions [214] that localises by matching the contour of the horizon to a model derived from an elevation map. Lebegue and Aggarwal [139] presented a system based on a similar method

---

[2] Models and representation for computer vision are discussed in the next section.

of straight-line matching as used in the outdoor urban system. This was applied to indoor environments, based on the assumption that significant objects have parallel lines with known 3-D orientations with respect to a global coordinate system (e.g., doorways). For localisation in nuclear power plants, the system of Ebihara, Otani, and Kume [67] matches solid flat rectangular objects in the environment. For the update problem when the initial position is known, the Extended Kalman Filter is frequently used to track position (e.g., [143, 234]). Other researchers have used probabilistic methods for localisation (e.g., [110, 204]) where the initial location is not known.

Docking

For mobile robots to operate on objects, such as assembly operations [127], or plugging into a recharging socket, robots often need to dock with the object. This involves moving close enough to the object to perform an operation, or possibly physically interfacing with the object (e.g., grasping an object handle with a manipulator).

Docking is often performed in two phases: initially the robot moves close to the object using sensory feedback; once the robot is close, it moves carefully into the final position. The initial motion can be relatively fast, and can utilise vision-based processing, whereas the fine positioning must be executed with care because of the likelihood of collision, it is often performed by optical and mechanical proximity sensors [186]. For operations such as assembly, an alternative to fine positioning is possible, whereby the robot manipulator trajectories are adjusted to take account of mobile robot docking errors [154].

For vision-based docking, there are both frame-based and active approaches. We present examples of both types.

Arkin and MacKenzie [5] use object recognition based on a constrained Hough transform [229]. Having recognised the object, the system extracts approximate object pose based on a target region of the object of known size and position. This pose estimate is then used to guide robot motion for docking. In order to transform the model, the Hough method requires an estimate of relative object location, which must be accurate to within several feet.

Santos-Victor and Sandini [195] present an active docking behaviour that defines robot goals in a manner that enables direct visual servoing for docking, see Figure 2.1. Visual servoing uses visual feedback directly for closed-loop robot control [113]. The goals are that the robot should adjust its direction so that the camera optical axis is aligned with the surface normal, and approach speed should decrease as the robot moves close to the object. Robot motion is derived directly by first-order space time derivatives of image motion across the image sequence. An advantage of this type of active approach is that it does not require calibration of the setup. Murphy and Arkin [162] also present a technique that moves towards landmarks by tracking landmark features during motion.

 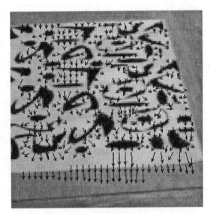

Figure 2.1: The flow-based docking system of Santos-Victor and Sandini. The images show the system approaching a textured docking surface, and a sample of the normal flow field used to estimate the motion parameters. Courtesy Jose Santos-Victor and Guilio Sandini, reprinted with permission from Santos-Victor and Sandini, "Visual Behaviours for Docking" [195].

All of these techniques assume that the robot is facing the surface of the object with which it has to dock, and implicitly assume some other mechanism that will bring the robot to such a point. There is a lack of research in systems that can dock with objects that are approached from any angle.

Obstacle detection and avoidance

A robot must be able to cope with the appearance of unexpected obstacles in order to navigate safely through an environment. To support robot motion at a reasonable speed, these methods must operate quickly. To achieve this research groups have developed methods that make strong assumptions about the type of environment and obstacle, as well as the geometry of the problem. Most object detection methods are based around one of two assumptions: a uniform ground characteristic; or the ground-plane assumption.

The uniform ground characteristic assumption is suitable for ground-planes of relatively uniform intensity, colour, or texture. In this case large regions of pixels that do not share this characteristic can be treated as obstacles. Horswill [108] used a uniform intensity assumption, and thus take the presence of an edge in the image to indicate an obstacle in the environment. Using a camera that is fixed to the robot, pointing in front of the robot at an angle to the ground, camera images can be transformed based on calibration so that the position of the edge in the image indicates the position of the obstacle relative to the robot. For this calibration to be effective, objects must be sitting on the ground without any excessive overhang. Further, objects must be of different intensity to the ground, and pieces of paper on the floor, rough edges in carpet, or even shadows may be interpreted as obstacles. A similar method for detecting obstacles was the basis of an obstacle avoidance system by Ku and Tsai [134]. Figure 2.2 shows a similar diagram to that used by Ku and Tsai to illustrate the image plane to ground plane transform.

In the ground-plane assumption, any regions that are not in the plane defined by the ground are considered to be obstacles, see Figure 2.2. To exploit this assumption some means of discriminating ground-plane points from points not in the ground plane is required. However, traditional vision methods involving 3-D reconstruction are not generally fast enough to support robot navigation. Typical approaches use qualitative stereo or optical flow. Stereo methods require some feature points to match between images, generally edges. Optical flow-based methods require some form of surface texture on obstacles.

Qualitative stereo-based obstacle detection methods generally either assume a calibrated ground plane, or estimate the equation of the plane in some way. The computation required to assess whether points are within this plane or not is much simpler than that required to find the true 3-D location of the points. Xie [239] presents a qualitative stereo method that transforms a known ground-plane into the image plane in both images. Under this transformation features within the ground plane will have zero disparity. Image regions with apparent disparity indicate the space occupied by obstacles. Zhang, Weiss, and Hanson [242] present two qualitative stereo-based algorithms, and one

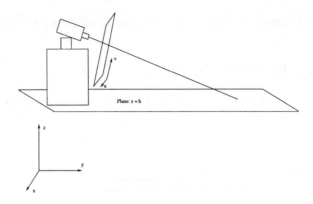

Figure 2.2: For a calibrated robot setup, a transform can be calculated that allows a robot system to infer the 3D position of points on the ground plane in robot centred coordinates (x,y,z) from the image coordinates (u,v). Based on the uniform characteristic assumption, the position of any non-uniform region in robot coordinates can be calculated based on its position in the image. Systems using the ground-plane detect if any regions fall outside the ground plane, and thus infer obstacle positions.

that is partially quantitative. In the first algorithm they assume a calibrated ground plane. The second estimates the location of the ground plane. The known ground plane algorithm outperforms the estimated ground plane algorithm when the plane is accurately known. Their final method allows for the ground-plane to change over time, updating the estimated ground plane using a Kalman filter. This method calculates the height of points above the estimated ground plane, and uses some camera calibration, so is partly a quantitative stereo method. The method assumes that there is no translation between the cameras in the direction of the focal axis and that the height above a reference ground plane of one camera is known.

Santos-Victor and Sandini [193] present an optical flow-based obstacle detection method. They assume that the robot is moving on ground floor and that any object not lying in this plane is an obstacle. By inverse projection of the flow vector field on the ground plane, points that are not on the ground-plane will be clear by their optical flow pattern. Knowledge of vehicle motion and camera intrinsic parameters is not required. Sull and Sridhar [211] have applied an optical-flow-based technique to detect obstacles on a runway from flying vehicles.

2.2.2 Mobile robot object recognition

Although there has been a great deal of research on general object recognition, little attention has been paid to object recognition specifically for mobile robots. However, equipping mobile robots with object recognition has many benefits. If a robot can recognise a specified object it can perform deterministic actions with that object, rather than general navigation and exploration. As discussed earlier, the dominant approach to robot navigation is to have a representation of the environment and move to a goal point based on localisation. In order to interact with objects, localisation-based robots require knowledge of the object's pose and position with respect to the environment. This is not a robust behaviour if the object is not precisely aligned. For example, fork-lift robots for pallet handling will have difficulty picking up misaligned pallets if they cannot adjust based on the actual position [82].

Many robot navigation systems operate primarily by using range-based sensors. Such sensors are only able to discriminate objects with structural differences. When a robot is moving around an object, it is desirable for the system to be able to differentiate the object from background objects that may be structurally similar, this is illustrated in Figure 2.3. Some research has examined integrating range sensors with visual object recognition [121], but this approach has not yet been extensively applied for mobile robots.

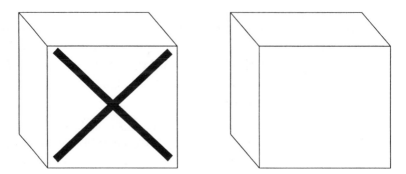

Figure 2.3: These two objects are structurally identical, but one has a clear marking that could be detected by a vision-based system.

The entrants in 'Clean Up the Tennis Court' and similar robot contests tend to make use of simple vision systems which are adequate for the specific task, but lack generality. For example, the system used by Sargent, Bailey, Witty, and Wright [196] can track multiple objects as long as they can be distinguished by colour.

Of the systems that are able to recognise a broader class of objects, some only apply two-dimensional (2D) techniques [40, 127]. For example, the KAMRO system [127] recognises and locates workpieces placed on a workbench. The system is adequate for objects placed on a set surface with an overhead camera, where only 2D projection is required. However, the system is unsuitable if the camera can view the object from many different angles.

There have been a few systems that recognise objects based on a full 3D approach. For instance, the system by Arkin and MacKenzie [5], described earlier, uses object recognition based on a constrained Hough transform [229]. The system cannot handle approaching the object from any angle and requires an initial estimate of its position.

In traditional object recognition, and in robot navigation generally, present systems for object recognition are inadequate for the task of guiding a mobile robot around a diverse range of objects.

2.2.3   Maps and path planning

The classical approach to path planning for mobile robot navigation performs precise planning and attempts to find optimal paths. It is based on the assumption of complete and precise knowledge of the environment and precise robot motion, see [199] for examples. Such assumptions have been found to be unworkable in many practical situations. Various authors, including Brooks [27] have pointed out inadequacies of this approximation. For instance, the world is inherently 3D, even if the robot moves in only 2D: objects may be small enough for the robot to see over, but not travel over, similarly objects may over-hang the workspace allowing the robot to pass under them, but may obscure landmarks. Further, global or absolute coordinate systems often are not appropriate. Although, errors in dead-reckoning have solutions such as landmarks, these are not appropriate for all situations. Finally, there are problems with modelling real-world environments, especially as polyhedra.

Of more recent path planning research, much is performed using either configuration-space, or potential field-based approaches. The configuration-space approach [147, 148] in mobile robots can be seen as expanding object boundaries by the robot's radius and shrinking the object to a point. Thus, the free-space [26] that can be traversed by the robot can be found. This method generally assumes that the environment is known [116]. The potential field approach for manipulators can be stated as follows:

> The manipulator moves in a field of forces. The position to be reached is an attractive pole for the end effector and obstacles are repulsive surfaces for the manipulator parts. [128]

The translation of this to mobile robots is straightforward. Potential fields are a local approach and so can have difficulties with local minima.

Ballistic and controlled motion

Arkin and Murphy [6] distinguish between two types of mobile robot motion. Firstly, *ballistic motion* is a smooth continuous motion performed in an open loop manner based on anticipatory perception. *Controlled motion* is performed in a closed-loop manner, where robot speed is dependent on the speed of perception. It may include periods of inaction during planning. Ballistic motion is typically performed in approaching the object, then controlled motion is required for the final approach interaction, particularly for docking.

2.2.4   Temporal sequencing for complex tasks

Temporal sequencing of algorithms for different tasks can facilitate complex behaviour [5]. For instance, a robot is initially guided towards a desired object. When it recognises the object [229] a transition occurs, and the robot moves close based on object properties. Then, ultrasound guides docking once the object is too close for visual feedback.

2.2.5   Vision-guided mobile robot systems

Having introduced some basic techniques for robotic navigation, the following sections present complete mobile robot systems.

Map learning and navigation

Recent research has seen two distinct approaches to mobile robot navigation based on maps: grid-based and topological. Firstly, *grid-based* methods divide the environment up into evenly spaced cells, and assign a value representing confidence that an obstacle is present in that location [22, 72, 73, 172]. These cells may be three-dimensional volume elements (*voxels*). In such a method building the map is relatively straight-forward. However, grid-based methods generate very complex maps which lead to complexity for planning, and large representations [221]. *Topological approaches* represent the environment by graphs, where nodes correspond to distinct situations or locations, and arcs connect nodes if a direct path exists between them [135]. The locations are often identified by landmarks as discussed above. Symbolic planners and problem solvers can be used with topological maps, and so planning can be performed more easily. However, topological methods can have difficulty determining whether places that look alike are the same location, particularly when they are reached from different directions, and may have trouble recognising geometrically close places. Further, topological maps are difficult to construct for large environments [221]. Grid-based methods, however, do not suffer from these problems.

Thrun [221] presented a method which combines grid-based and topological approaches and avoids some pitfalls of each. The method builds a topological map on top of a grid-based map using Voronoi diagrams [37] by splitting the grid-based map into coherent regions separated by what Thrun calls critical lines, which correspond to narrow passages, such as doorways. The method retains the ease of construction of grid-based representations, however, the topological approach also makes path planning between regions efficient. Unfortunately, the large memory requirements of the grid-based approach remains.

Another approach uses Markov models to represent a probability distribution over all possible robot locations and updates the distribution based on new evidence using Bayes' rule [204]. The method also combines topological and metric information, but assumes that the topological data and some metric data is provided.

2.2.6   Reactive navigation

Brooks [30] developed the idea of *behaviour-based robots*. He proposed
that complete internal representations of the external environment are
not necessary for agents to act in a competent manner [31]. Brooks
also proposed that intelligence is determined by the dynamics of interaction with the world, quoting Simon's [205] example of the apparently
complex behaviour of an ant walking along a beach is more a reflection of environment complexity than the ant's own internal complexity. Thus, intelligent behaviour may be emergent from the interaction
of simple modules and the environment. This is the basis of the well-
known subsumption architecture [29], which uses layers of modules.
The low-level layers are entirely reactive, performing tasks such as obstacle avoidance, while higher-level modules select a goal to navigate
towards, and allow low-level reactive layer to take care of avoiding collisions. Between layers there is no central locus of control or central
representation. Subsumption architecture-based systems have proven
capable of demonstrating what has been traditionally seen as higher
forms of intelligence such as learning [151].

   An example of a system developed based on the subsumption architecture is described by Horswill and Brooks [109]. The system can
follow arbitrarily moving objects guided by vision. It performs simple
tracking of blobs over images at about 5 frames/second. The motor
control reacts to the object position to keep the blob centred in the
image by rotating and advancing the robot based on the blob's x,y
offset from the image centre. Further, the obstacle detection system of
Horswill [108] described above, forms part of a reactive solution to obstacle avoidance. Reactive control turns the robot toward the direction
of the greatest freespace.

2.2.7   Model-based vision systems for mobile robots

A model for a vision system is some form of representation of things of
interest that the system make expect to appear. Models are discussed
in more detail in the next section. Through the use of models, systems
may be able to perform more complex interactions than simple navigation and obstacle avoidance, and may achieve more reliable behaviour
in specific environments. Models often make systems more specific to
environments and tasks as they represent particular things, although
these may be broad categories of environments and tasks.

The behaviour-based approach [30] states that the environment is its own best model. However, Thrun [220] argues that while the environment is certainly its most accurate model, to be useful a model must be accessible, and the environment is often not easily accessible. The trade-off between composed model and self-model for the environment depends on the ratio of the robot's perceptual range relative to the size of its environment. Thus, systems with models scale better to a more complex environment than those without.

Tsubouchi and Yuta [225] present a model-based matching navigation system that match between an abstraction of a real image and an image that is generated from an environmental map to navigate in an indoor office environment. The system makes use of high level features in its matching: it matches trapezoids in the environment, and checks that they are on objects of correct colour. In this system, localisation corresponds to view recognition in model-based object recognition. The system recognises a particular configuration of trapezoids as corresponding to a particular location. More exact position information is extracted by correspondence between the geometric shape observed, and that modelled.

More recently, authors such as Dulimarta and Jain [63] have used more extensive models for vision-based navigation. Their system operates in indoor office environments, it recognises doors and corners, and counts ceiling lights to localise. The system uses template matching to recognise digits on door plates. All door plates are at approximately the same height in the system's environment. The list of possible candidate door plates is small for the update problem.

2.2.8   Knowledge-based mobile robotic systems

In order to complete complex tasks it is often necessary to have knowledge about the environment, the tasks required, and objects that tasks will be performed on. Further, in practical applications, *a priori* domain knowledge about the environment and task can be used to limit computational complexity, and make measurements more robust [100].

The University of Karlsruhe developed KAMRO (Karlsruhe Autonomous Mobile Robot), a robot system for manufacturing environments [186]. The system uses knowledge-based planning performed by several expert systems to perform navigation and assembly tasks. The plans are at a high level, such as, move to the appropriate location, and then perform an operation. The system also uses functional and technical information on the parts that are to be assembled. Tasks to be performed by the assembly component [102] are described by a set of precedent constraints, modelled as a Condition/Event Petri net. The robot knowledge base is stored using a frame system.

Marti, Batlle, and Casals [156] describe a rule-based robotic platform for recognising objects for an industrial environment. The system's environmental model makes strong assumptions about how this particular type of industrial environment can appear. Specifically, that parallel lines will meet at a distant vanishing point, and that objects can be described as sticks and blobs. Object recognition is achieved through combination of evidence: using knowledge of the segmentation process; spatial relationships between primitives in the scene; model compositional knowledge; and, how to combine model compositions into complete scene interpretations.

2.2.9   Vision-guided mobile robots using stereo

Stereo correspondence is computationally expensive, and thus not extensively applied in mobile robotic systems, as discussed earlier, qualitative stereo has seen some application recently. However, there are a number of systems have used stereo. Stereo has the advantage that it does not require an environmental model to calculate range.

Braunegg [23] proposes an indoor navigation system that recognises the room it is in, and its position and orientation in the room. The system uses stereo to find long near-vertical edges in intensity images. The system aggregates images across a 360° rotation of the room. The authors propose that such features usually correspond to objects that do not tend to move, and thus are suitable for localisation. The features are projected into the ground plane to form an occupancy-grid model. Burschka and Farber [35] construct a model of indoor environments by exploration using binocular stereo. A multi-layer map stores the 3D boundary lines of objects at geometrical positions in the world. Tucakov and Lowe [226] present a method that overcomes some of the computational problems of stereo by anticipating changes in stereo depth maps over a time sequence of images. A significant amount of early research in stereo for mobile robot navigation, including visual map making, has been developed at INRIA [8, 9].

2.2.10   Active perception systems for mobile robots

The active perception paradigm considers that perception is intimately related to the physiology of the perceiver and the tasks that it performs [3]. Although, early active vision research was concerned with *general recovery*[3] [4], active perception is more closely related to purposive and animate vision. In Purposive vision, vision is seen as part of a complex system that interacts in specific ways with the world [3]. The function of vision is to support this interaction. Animate vision insists that vision is more readily understood in the context of the visual behaviours in which the system is engaged [10]. Animate vision emphasises the advantages of techniques such as fixation, where the camera motion is controlled so that a fixated point is constantly imaged to the same point in the image plane [185]. This can be used to: determine relative range; verify range; stabilise a camera on a moving platform; and analyse hidden surfaces on an object. The paradigm has been defined as follows:

> An active visual system is a system which is able to manipulate its visual parameters in a controlled manner in order to extract useful data about the scene in space and time. [174]

Although active perception is a relatively new form of computer vision, a number of successful active perception mobile robot systems exist. The research in this area is predominantly concerned with specific applications under particular assumptions, and is not typically characterised by large integrated systems. The research of two particularly prominent laboratories is outlined to exemplify active vision for mobile robots.

The LIRA Lab.

The Integrated Laboratory for Advanced Robotics (LIRA-Lab.) has produced a number of applications of active perception for mobile robots. Santos-Victor and Sandini [194] present three systems that work solely with partial information from the image flow field as input and heading direction and velocity as control variables. Their method embeds in navigation behaviours the perceptual processes necessary to understand the aspects of the environment required to generate purposeful motor output. This relies on a purposive definition of the task

---

[3]General vision is discussed later in this review.

which is solved by a behaviour. The behaviours presented are: a centring reflex for moving along corridors or following walls; detection of obstacles on the floor (described above); and, docking (described above).

The centring reflex is achieved by *divergent stereo*, where two cameras point laterally, and simultaneous images are acquired to the left and right of the robot during motion. The system uses two closed loops: a navigation loop controls rotation speed to balance the left and right optical flows; and, a velocity loop controls the forward speed by accelerating/decelerating as a function of the amplitude of the lateral flow fields. The velocity loop is intended to link the robot speed directly to the size of the environment, which is presented in detail in [192]. Divergent stereo was initially proposed as the mechanism that enables bees to fly down the centre of a tunnel [207]. It has also been implemented by other groups as a means for navigation [206].

The LIRA lab has also performed robot navigation which exploits the log-polar sensor. The log-polar sensor [184] is a CCD camera with a non-uniform resolution across the sensor, it has high resolution at the fovea, and low-resolution at the peripheral part of the image. The log-polar mapping samples at n evenly spaced angles around the sensor at m radii. Thus, the elements appear in co-centric circles, and are increasingly large toward the periphery. Images can be taken by resampling a Cartesian image, or using a CMOS implementation of the device [184]. On mobile robots the LIRA lab has demonstrated the computational advantages of such a mapping for the calculation of time-to-impact with approaching obstacles, which can be useful for problems such as the docking problem [222].

Yale University

Hager [90] developed a general purpose substrate for real-time vision-based robotics. This software system provides tracking modules for tracking image features including edges, corners and blobs. This system provides the basis for building systems for visual servoing [93]. Recently, Hager and Belhumer [92] presented a region-based tracking method that overcomes some previous limitations of tracking. The system can track objects under non-affine changes in pose relative to the camera, occlusion, and changes in illumination. The method is based on minimising the sum-of-squared differences between regions in images, which is an established tracking technique. A reference image is taken at time zero. The system handles affine warping by allowing a parametric motion model for change from reference images over time. Changes in illumination are handled by taking a set of bias images under different illumination conditions. From a linear combination of these it is possible to generate an image under novel lighting conditions, assuming there is no self-shadowing. Occlusions are handled by rejecting portions of the tracked region that cause high errors in the estimation process.

Hager, Kriegman, Yeh, and Rasmussen [91] have also applied edge-based tracking to the standard localisation problem, using an active vision approach. From initial self-location, they use visual tracking to extend the definitions of place to a range of locations. The system requires that nearly all of the world corresponds to some place. The system uses the continuity of the representation to predict changes of view between places, thereby eliminating the need for a strong notion of navigation. Also, the system can be programmed simply by showing it the required path.

Other active perception research

Mittal, Valilaya, Banerjee, and Balakrishnan [161] present a divergent optical flow system for avoiding possible collisions with approaching objects, as well as stationary objects when the robot is moving. The system uses first order derivatives of optical flow to determine bounds on time-to-collision. The frame rate restricts the speeds that can be handled as movements between frames must be infinitesimal for flow equation to be valid. Also, the system requires that the visible surface is essentially planar, that there is no occlusion, and that depth range is small compared to viewing distance.

Janabi-Sharifi and Wilson [118] point out that the performance of visual servoing systems is highly affected by the selected features. Features may become occluded, move out of the field of view, or provide weak information that may lead to task failure. They present a system for automatic CAD-based feature and window selection for visual servoing using the extended Kalman filter. The authors derive two sets of constraints on the visibility and motion of features. The first set is task constraints imposed by the geometry of the workspace, while the second set consists of feature extraction and pose estimation constraints. The latter are useful for evaluating potential features or feature sets for visual servoing. The constraints are applied in order to reduce the dimensionality of the feature sets for automatic feature selection. The paper does not present experiments where features are dynamically updated, such as, when the view of an object moves around a corner so that all previous features become occluded and features of the new surface become visible.

2.2.11 Application of vision-guided mobile robots

Road vehicles

The application of vision guided techniques to road vehicles is one of the most extensively explored areas of mobile robot navigation. This is partly due to research by the Carnegie Mellon University (CMU) Robotics Institute, and some other notable systems. Here discussion is restricted to systems that aim to control the steering of road vehicles to follow roads, or follow a leading car.

Over a period of many years, CMU developed a series of vehicle systems [219]. The SCARF (Supervised Classification Applied to Road Following) system [45] uses colour vision to steer the vehicle for road following. It classifies pixels as either road or non-road, and uses a Hough voting scheme to fit a triangular model to the road. It is robust to poor road edges, hence is able to follow less structured roads, and is tolerant of shadows across roads. It is implemented on a specially designed supercomputer [46]. Earlier road-following systems were intolerant of a lack of road structure. For example, the system of Dickmanns and Grafe [56, 57] is able to achieve speeds of up to 100kph on the German autobarn, but relies on the road's smooth curves, known widths, and clear markings.

More recently CMU has further developed this research, and produced the system RALPH (Rapidly Adapting Lateral Position Handler) [182], which supported a vehicle driving at up to 91 mph for 3000 miles in total. Figure 2.4 shows images from the system. The system steered autonomously 96% of the way on one particular section of 302 miles. CMU has also developed a neural network-based system [181] to accomplish lane transitions [122].

The task of following other cars has attracted considerable attention recently. This enables a platoon of cars to drive together, with full control only required for the lead car. Du and Papanikolopoulos [62] employed a symmetry axis detection scheme that detects contour symmetry to compute a bounding box around the leading vehicle, with

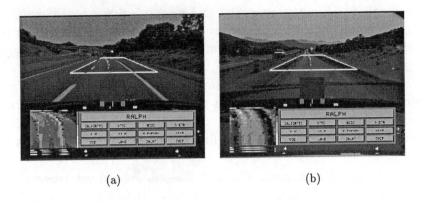

(a)   (b)

Figure 2.4: Images from CMU's RALPH road following system. The trapezoid shows the the region of the image used for road-following, which is resampled to eliminate the effects of perspective [51]. (a) Approaching a corner. (b) Tracking a road under construction. Courtesy of Charles Thorpe.

similar work performed by [244]. Further, there has been research into tracking road vehicles from cameras placed above the road [81, 87, 131] for interpreting the actions of cars in an intersection [48].

Industrial Robots

The current state-of-the-art in industrial robots is characterised by robots that do not make extensive use of perception performing fixed repeated tasks. However, there are a number of groups developing autonomous vehicles specifically for manufacturing tasks including assembly, navigation in industrial environments, and pallet moving. We examples below.

Early work on the manufacturing system KAMRO was discussed above. A more recent version of the system [150] consists of a two-armed mobile robot that can: perform assembly tasks without human intervention; move collision-free between workstations; and, locate and assemble parts. The system uses a combination of sensors, namely, ultra-sonics, laser-range finder, and stereo vision. This system is able to move the platform in combination with the manipulators in order to achieve longer trajectories than non-mobile robot arm systems.

Other systems focus on autonomous navigation in industrial environments, for instance, Pages, Aranda, and Casals [173] describe a mobile robot system that navigates and generates maps, based on high-speed dynamic stereo. The system takes advantage of the structure of this particular industrial environment by only considering straight lines. Collins, Henshaw, Arkin, and Webster [42] present a system for autonomous robot navigation to support routine monitoring in hazardous environments. The system is able to navigate reliably along aisles, through the adaptation of successful road following techniques, using the fast line finder [125] to find the edges in order to follow a path.

Garibotto, Masciangelo, Ilic, and Bassino [82] added sensory capability and local intelligence to a conventional fork lift. The system is able to perform a complete autonomous mission including a series of transportation phases of pallet loading/unloading. H-shaped landmarks on the floor facilitate localisation. The system uses model-based computer vision to identify pallets and their pose based on the central cavities, making the system tolerant of slightly misplaced pallets.

Space robotics

The Mars Pathfinder mission has given a dramatic and very well publicised demonstration of the potential of robots for planetary exploration [158]. There are considerable benefits in removing the need for people to be present on space missions: it greatly reduces the risk of loss of life; and reduces mission costs (e.g., robots need not return to earth). Research into autonomous planetary navigation has been underway for some time: the Jet Propulsion Laboratory began developing rovers[4] in the 1970's [218]. Fully teleoperated robots are impractical for planetary exploration as round-trip communication times to Mars, approximately between 6-45 minutes, would make progress slow [235]. Thus, some degree of autonomous action is certainly required. Vision is preferable over active sensors due to power efficiency and reliability requirements [236]. Path planning required for Martian terrain is more complex than for most existing mobile robots that operate in structured environments, as traversability is a continuous quantity [84].

Krotov, Herbert, and Simmons [133] present a prototype lunar rover using stereo perception and dead reckoning. A system for automatic mountain detection and pose estimation for the teleoperation has also

---

[4]Vehicles for exploring the surface of the moon and other planets are often referred to as *rovers*.

been developed for the rover [44]. The system aims to present position estimates for to a ground-based operator based on the position of detected mountains. This is intended to increase situational awareness and prevent loss of orientation for the operator. A Russian rover has also been developed incorporating a navigation based on stereo produced by the French space agency CNES [138].

Stieber, Trudel, and Hunter [208] review mission and tasks to be performed by external robotic devices on the international space station. They also present an overview of the design of the Mobile Servicing System for the station, which is a large arm with small dextrous manipulators at the end of it (the small manipulators are effectively on a mobile platform).

In [74], Erickson, Grimm, Pendleton, Howard, Goode, Hawkins, Bloss, Seaborn, Hess, Walker, Phinney, Norsworthy, Anderson, Chien, Hewgill, Littleford, and Gaudiano present the early stages of development of a prototype supervised intelligent robot to: hold objects for the crew, retrieve/replace tools and other objects from/into storage; and retrieve objects or crew that have become separated from the craft. The robot will use visual perception to recognise, locate, and keep track of objects.

Agricultural robots

Many application systems have been developed for agriculture, including automatic guidance systems, and fruit-harvesting robots [68]. Guidance systems are generally restricted to simple tasks such as finding the next line of fruit trees to be picked or following crop lines [21, 94]. One example of a fruit harvesting system, particularly melon-picking [68] employs a Cartesian manipulator mounted on a mobile chassis. Vision sensors locate fruit and guide a gripper towards it to pick the melon. The system uses vision, odometry, and GPS to follow crop rows.

2.3   Computer Vision for Mobile Robots

Much of the literature in computer vision addresses the general vision problem [155], that is developing vision methods that are appropriate for all situations, tasks and environments. At the other end of the spectrum is the work that solves specific problems using methods that do not generalise.

The use of computer vision in this book is specific to mobile robots. The specific methods presented are general to a class of mobile robots, but the principles are intended to be general to all mobile robots. As such, this section presents computer vision literature that is seen as being most relevant to mobile robotics. There is a good deal of fundamental research in computer vision that will not be presented here because of space constraints, and extensive previous coverage, including [2, 89, 97, 98, 106, 104, 155, 190, 191, 202, 241], The reader is referred to these and other texts on computer vision and digital image processing for fundamental computer vision concepts and techniques. This chapter also presents literature on high-level vision methods that are used in this book, namely object recognition and shape-from-shading. As mobile robots act in a 3D world, this section is restricted predominantly to 3D vision systems.

2.3.1 Traditional model-based vision 3D object recognition

In order to recognise an object, a system requires some form of representation, or model, of the object. Typically, this describes criteria that must be satisfied in order for the system to determine that the object is present in the scene. It may also give other information about the object, that is relevant to subsequent actions that the system must perform. There are two main categories of object recognition system based on the way objects are represented: viewer-centred or object-centred. Viewer-centred representations model the object as it appears in an image, by a (possibly large) number of views. It may be necessary to match many candidate views to find the correct one. Alternatively, object-centred representations model the object in three dimensions. Thus, either 3D reconstruction must be performed on the image, or the object model must be rendered to compare it to images.

Real-time processing is a major constraint on any vision system to be used for mobile robots. It is often unacceptable for the robot to pause frequently for long periods of processing between actions, although it may be acceptable in exceptional cases. Both object-centred and viewer-centred representations have real-time processing limitations.

Object-centred representations

There are many forms of object-centred representation for object recognition, some of the more commonly used are: wire-frames; volumetric techniques and sweep representations; Constructive Solid Geometry (CSG); Surface Models (B-Reps)/Surface-Edge-Vertex representations; and, spatial occupancy enumeration. Surveys and detailed descriptions of 3D object-centred representation schemes can be found in [79, 98, 187, 232].

Early vision systems such as [189] used wire-frame models to match polyhedral objects where only edges are represented. Wire-frame models cannot represent surface shape, and have been shown to be ambiguous even for plane-faced solids [187].

ACRONYM [25] represented 3D objects using generalised cones (also known as generalised cylinders, or sweep representations.) Generalised cones are formed by taking a curve (spline) in 2D space and sweeping it about a constant angle to the tangent of the spline, while deforming according to a deformation function. Objects are modelled as subpart hierarchies using a frame-based representations. Frames are discussed below.

Biederman [20] proposed a qualitative object representation called geons (geometrical ions). Geons also represent objects by part as a collection of generalised-cone components, but do not make use of quantitative representation. Biederman proposed a catalogue of 36 geons that can be readily discriminated based on differences in nonaccidental properties among generalised cones. Combining a few geon subparts rapidly leads to a very large number of objects that can be represented when possible comparative sizes and connection relationships are considered. Geons have been successfully applied to computer object recognition [54].

Constructive Solid Geometry (CSG) was introduced by Requincha [188]. In CSG, an object is represented by a collection of primitives (e.g., cuboids, pyramids, cylinders, cones and spheres), a set of transformations (e.g., translation, rotation, and scaling) and boolean operations (e.g., union, intersection, and difference). The composition of these primitives is called a CSG tree.

PREMIO (PREdiction in Matching Images to Objects) [36] makes use of a surface-edge-vertex representation, which are similar to BReps in computer graphics. The representation contains a list of surfaces, edges, and vertices of the object, and topological relations between these entities.

Occupancy-based representations represent a solid by enumeration of its spatial occupancy. The cells are commonly called *voxels* (volume elements) and are cubes in a fixed spatial grid. Occupancy based representations are commonly used in mobile robot mapping as discussed earlier.

Viewer-centred representations

Aspect graphs exemplify the basic ideas of viewer-centred representations. The aspect graph was originally proposed by Koenderink and Van Doorn [130]. Aspect graphs enumerate every possible characteristic view of an object. A *characteristic view* is a continuous region of views, for which all the visible edges and vertices, together with their connectivity relationships are the same [233]. Thus, neighbouring characteristic views are distinguished by a change in the object's visual feature topology, called a *visual event*. Characteristic views are general in the sense that a continuous range of viewpoints around the object is represented by a single view. In an aspect graph, each characteristic view is represented by a node, and a visual event is represented by an edge between neighbouring nodes.

Precise formal definitions of aspect graph-like representations differ, for example, in the importance assigned to visual events [231], and whether a continuous path of points is required between viewpoints of a single characteristic view [233]. However, the basic idea of representing a three-dimensional object by a set of two-dimensional characteristic views remains consistent across researchers.

An object may be modelled under orthographic projection, in which case there is only a two-dimensional view-sphere of possible object viewing locations. Otherwise, if perspective projection is taken into account, there is a three-dimensional space of possible focus points around the object from which it can be viewed, incorporating distance from the object as a parameter. In either case, the region of viewspace over which an aspect, or characteristic view is visible is called a Characteristic View Domain [41, 231]. Aspect graph-type representations have been derived for polyhedra [86, 233], planar-faced solids [231], quadric-surfaced solids [41], curved objects with algebraic surfaces [179], and solids of revolution [69, 70].

Aspect graphs have problems of practicality [76]. The *scale problem* is that the visual events differentiating views can occur at a very large or microscopic scale. The number of nodes in an aspect graph for a real object can easily reach several million, and many of these may be irrelevant at the scale at which observations will be made. The *indexing problem* follows from the large number of views. Matching each view in turn is clearly time-consuming, and the problem compounds further with multiple object databases.

There have been subsequent proposals that assist in controlling some of these problems. Eggert, Bowyer, Dyer, Christensen, and Goldof [71] tackle the scale problem by defining a scale space aspect graph. This provides a mechanism for selecting a sufficient level of detail for explicit representation. Ben-Arie [16] defines a visibility sphere method, and presents probabilistic models for viewed angles and distances. This method can be used to compute observation probabilities for an object's aspects. Probabilistic weighting, and restricting an initial recognition to only the most likely views, eases indexing problems somewhat. Other research implemented hierarchical indexing for viewer-centred object representations [33].

Other researchers have proposed viewer-centred models that are not aspect graph variations. For example, Ullman and Basri [227] propose recognition by matching image features to linear combinations of a base set of two-dimensional views of the object.

Recent approaches

Dickinson, Pentland, and Rosenfeld [54] model objects for recognition as compounds of a finite set of volumetric part classes, simplifying object database indexing. In [55], this is applied to recognise objects for the purpose of guiding a robot arm. However, this method is only applicable to objects composed of distinct volumetric parts [52, 53].

The indexing and scale problems have been contained somewhat by recent variations on two-dimensional modelling. However, the problems still remain for recognising an object from a large database, when the pose of the object in the image is unknown, and no cues are available. This can be seen as part of the problem with general vision.

2.3.2 Shape-from-shading

Shape-from-shading is the process of recovering the three-dimensional shape of the underlying scene from a two-dimensional image. The classical computer vision [155] approach attempts to build a model of a three-dimensional scene from a single image. Most shape-from-shading research takes this classical approach, where examples are shown in [106]. However, it is well known that shape-from-shading is underdetermined and difficult to solve, certainly, simplifications are necessary. For instance, the light source and observer are assumed to be far from the object, and the underlying surface is Lambertian . All works impose some constraints. For example, typical *variational* approaches to the shape-from-shading problem, such as that of Brooks and Horn [24], require that the underlying surface be smooth, the albedo[5] be uniform across the scene, and *boundary conditions* are required. Boundary conditions are points where the surface normal can be determined to find a unique solution. Ikeuchi and Horn first pointed out that at the occluding (limb) boundary for smoothly curving surfaces, the surface normal is equal to the normal to the edge of the surface in the image plane. The assumption of the existence of an occluding limb boundary is common in shape-from-shading research, including [24, 32, 142, 152]. Most variational method papers use singular points to derive boundary conditions as well as limb boundaries, see [115] for an example. A singular point is a point where the brightness is maximal, indicating that the surface normal is in the direction of the light source. Ikeuchi and Horn [115] also show that in some cases, self-shadow boundaries can be used as singular points. In an early work in this area, Horn [103] derived a method of characteristic strips, where the shape is traced along characteristic strips of the image from a singular point. Oliensis [170] demonstrates that if there is at least one singular point, then there is a unique surface corresponding to the image. Dupuis and Oliensis [65] propose an algorithm that is able to find the shape of objects quickly when one or more singular points are visible. Local methods have to make other assumptions, and do not generally produce exact estimates of shape. For instance, Pentland [176], and Lee and Rosenfeld [141] assume that the surface is locally spherical. Although, Ferrie and Levine [77] have fewer restrictions, their method still requires local constraints on the surface geometry. Other works take a linear approximation to the reflectance model [178] that allows a closed form solution. However, this approximation is only accurate when the variation of surface normals in a region is small, or when the light source is oblique to the viewer. The linear approximation proposed in [223] does not handle

---

[5]Albedo is defined in [140] as the products of illumination and surface reflectivity at points on the surface.

noise well. To solve the shape-from-shading problem, Horn suggests [105] that it is necessary that the surface reflectance be locally uniform. However, the aim of reconstructing the shape of an arbitrary scene, with arbitrary lighting purely from image shading is probably not achievable even given this assumption.

Most of the research described above assumes that the surface for which shape is to be calculated has a Lambertian reflectance model, and is illuminated by a point source, thus the following relation holds:

$$I = N . S \qquad (2.1)$$

where I is the image irradiance at a particular point, N is the surface normal, and S is the direction of the light source. However, there has been a great deal of other research that has different lighting and reflectance models. For example, Horn and Sjoberg [107] derive the surface reflectance map in terms of the bidirectional reflectance-distribution function (BRDF) [167]. Based on this method, they derive reflectance functions for several special cases and show that image radiance is indirectly proportional to surface orientation. Nayar, Ikeuchi and Kanade [163] study surface reflectance models based on physical and geometrical optics. Geometrical models are based on the assumption that the wavelength of incident light is small compared with the dimensions of surface imperfections, so that physical models are more appropriate for smooth surfaces. They propose a reflectance framework to describe reflection of monochromatic light from surfaces that vary from rough to smooth. Schultz [198] presents a a technique called *specular stereo* that can recover the shape of a smooth specular surface under natural lighting from several images.

Implicit also in Equation 2.1 is the assumption of a known light source direction, and surface albedo. However, other authors discuss the estimation of these parameters. Pentland [177] presents a method for estimation of illuminant direction. The method assumes smooth Lambertian surface, a point light source, an umbilical surface, and that changes in the surface normal are isotropically distributed. However, this method only gives accurate slant estimation for a slant less than $40°$. Lee and Rosenfeld [141] improve the performance of slant estimation. The same authors [140] also derive a method for albedo estimation given a distant light source and Lambertian reflectivity. Finally, Zheng and Chellapa [243] presented a method that estimates illuminant direction and albedo, assuming uniform albedo and a smooth Lambertian surface. In this paper, two estimates of tilt angle were derived, the first was based on local estimates of smooth patches, the second used shading information along image contours. Illuminant slant and surface albedo were estimated from image statistics. Their methods are more robust and accurate than the earlier methods.

More recent work has brought an active approach to the shape-from-shading problem. Kutulakos and Dyer [136] purposefully control the motion of an active monocular observer to recover a global description of an object's shape.

Shape-from-shading solutions that utilise regularisation, and are based on the assumption of a limb-boundary, require that all of the surface be surrounded by a limb boundary. If boundary information is incomplete then the solution may not fully converge, but partial information may still be found [115].

Mathematical formulation

The shape-from-shading method presented in this book extends mathematical basis of the two papers [24, 152]. This work is described in some detail here as a context for later derivations.

Brooks and Horn [24] derived a method for finding the surface shape and light source direction for a smooth, Lambertian surface where boundary conditions are set. They use a global scheme based on the image irradiance equation with a smoothing component. The surface is found iteratively by minimising the error in the surface fit for a functional composed of the image irradiance equation, and a regularising term.

$$I(x,y) = \int \int_{\Omega} ((E - \mathbf{n} \cdot \mathbf{s})^2 + \lambda (\| \mathbf{n}_x \|^2 + \| \mathbf{n}_y \|^2) +$$
$$\mu(x,y)(\| \mathbf{n} \|^2 - 1)) dx dy, \qquad (2.2)$$

where E is the image irradiance, $\mu(x,y)$ is a Lagrange multiplier function to impose the constraint that $\mathbf{n}(x,y)$ is a unit vector, $\mathbf{s}$ points to the light source, $\mathbf{n}_x$ and $\mathbf{n}_y$ are the partial derivatives of n, and λ rates the relative importance of the regularisation term. Minimising I is solved as a problem of variational calculus. Brooks and Horn derive an iterative solution using the Euler equations.

Malik and Maydan [152] extend Brooks and Horn's technique by combining shape-from-shading with three-dimensional line drawing interpretation in order to find the shape from a single image with piece-wise smooth surfaces. They assume that the image has been pre-segmented, and that a sparse labelling of the image is available. The sparse labelling is used to constrain the object's possible shape. At a labelled vertex, with three or more visible surfaces, Malik and Maydan are typically able to constrain the surface normal at the points around the vertex to a unique value.

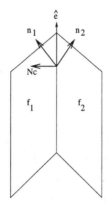

Figure 2.5: The tangent vector, and surface normals at a non-occluding edge.

Malik and Maydan extend Brooks and Horn's iterative scheme to propagate the shape across discontinuities. Let $\hat{e}$ be the unit tangent vector to the edge at a point on the roof, and let n_1 and n_2 be the unit surface normals to the tangent planes to the two faces f_1 and f_2 at that point, respectively. Let $\hat{e}$ be oriented such that when one walks on the edge in the direction of $\hat{e}$, the face f_1 is to the left (see Fig. 2.5). Now $\hat{e}$ is perpendicular to both n_1 and n_2, and thus parallel to $n_1 \times n_2$, provided that the edge's variation in depth is small compared to the distance between the surface and the camera. Also, let $\hat{e}_{proj}$ be the unit vector of the orthographic projection of $\hat{e}$ onto the image plane.

If we let N_c be a unit vector parallel to the image plane and perpendicular to $\hat{e}_{proj}$, then:

$$(n_1 \times n_2)_{proj} \cdot N_c = 0 \qquad (2.3)$$

We have four unknowns for the unit normals n_1 and n_2, of the two faces, and have only three equations: Eq. (2.3), and the image irradiance equation for the points on both surfaces. Thus, a unique solution is not possible. However, Malik and Maydan add a smooth-ness constraint and form a composite functional which allows shape to propagate across orientation discontinuities. Here the equation is formed for a general reflectance map $\mathbf{R}$ and is taken over the surface s:

$$I(x,y) = \int_s [\lambda_1[(E_1 - R(\mathbf{n_1}))^2 + ((E_2 - R(\mathbf{n_2}))^2] + \qquad (2.4)$$
$$\lambda_2[(\mathbf{n_1} \times \mathbf{n_2}) \cdot \mathbf{N_c}]^2 + \lambda_3(\| \mathbf{n_1'} \|^2 + \| \mathbf{n_2'} \|^2) +$$
$$\mu_1(\| \mathbf{n_1} \|^2 - 1) + \mu_2(\| \mathbf{n_2} \|^2 - 1)]ds$$

Again, the Euler equation of the composite functional is used to derive an iterative scheme for estimating the surface normal along a non-occluding edge.

The scheme operates by first constraining the surface normals at limbs, or vertices of three or more surfaces where all surfaces are show-ing. With these boundary conditions the scheme uses the method of [24] to propagate shape across surfaces, and the iterative method formed from Eq. (2.5) to propagate shape across orientation discontinuities.

Both these techniques require limb occluding boundaries, or singu-lar points to provide boundary conditions, and hence to find a unique solution. For smoothly curving surfaces, it is reasonable to assume that the use of these constraints will provide adequate boundary value con-ditions to calculate unique solutions for a large proportion of images. However, man-made objects often consist largely of flat surfaces. In such cases, there may not be a singular point where the surface normal is parallel to the light source. Also, there may not be any limbs, with all occluding edges possibly occurring at orientation discontinuities. Further, the scheme of Malik and Maydan [152] assumes that a sparse labelled edge diagram can be derived from edges extracted from a raw image. Edge labelling is not reliable with edges extracted from noisy image data. Further, they do not suggest a method for representing this knowledge.

Knowledge-based vision

The classical conception of computer vision, as illustrated in [155], ad-vocates a general vision that is appropriate for all situations, tasks and environments. This is based on the assumption that the human visual system is general. Human vision is more than adequate for moving our bodies around the environment consisting of features and objects that we are familiar with (or better again when it is an environment we have created), however, it is not general. Numerous psychological experiments have demonstrated the non-generality of the human visual system, for example, that human visual performance in recognising familiar objects degrades if the objects are seen out of context, [19]. In the case of shape, because humans can recognise the shape of objects quickly does not mean that general 3D surface reconstruction is being performed. Humans can utilise cues from knowledge of the objects being examined, and cues from other features of the environment to gain information required for successful completion of a task. It is seldom that human tasks require extraction of detailed 3D structure.

Similarly, for a robot to navigate around an environment, it does not require a vision system that recovers general information. For instance, rather than recovering the complete three-dimensional shape of an object, it may only be necessary to consider if the shape is consistent with that of the object the robot seeks. Further, if the robot has *a priori* information about its environment it should make full use of this information, not only for reasoning about which path to take, but also in the earliest stages of image interpretation. This book examines the application of knowledge-based methods to computer vision.

The importance of applying domain knowledge to artificial intelligence (AI) programs has been a fundamental observation arising from research into AI [78]. In computer vision, this observation has been applied to high-level computer vision, such as object recognition and scene interpretation [48, 60, 124], and to intermediate computer vision processes, such as segmentation [164, 203]. Other systems use rule-bases to make effective use of image processing operators for low and mid-level image analysis [157]. Lu [149] produced a knowledge-based system for detecting edges. However, in general, the use of knowledge for early vision processing has been restricted. Few systems use constraints from a knowledge-base directly in the operators, rather the knowledge-base is only used for controlling the application of the operators. Early vision processing has focussed on pre-cognitive methods where a generic operator is applied image based on some assumptions about the image formation process, and generic properties of what appears in the image.

Knowledge-based scene interpretation systems such as [60, 124, 146] emphasise application of symbolic knowledge to symbols which are extracted by low-level vision techniques. Also applying symbolic knowledge to control the application low-level vision techniques to direct computation toward relevant parts of the image. More recent work in this area also focuses on producing symbolic interpretation of scenes [59] and does not look at applying symbolic knowledge directly to numerical image operators.

Much of the research in knowledge-based systems has limited application to vision systems. Generally, knowledge-based approaches emphasise the role of purely symbolic inferencing for reasoning and decision-making [80]. However, much of the common-sense knowledge about problems is in the form of procedures or processes for achieving particular goals [85]. One important distinction between knowledge-based systems that reason about processes and those that reason about facts, is that processes may succeed or fail. For systems that interact in some way with an environment, such as vision systems, success or failure cannot be predicted. The result depends on the environment. It is often not adequate to take the standard logic programming approach of negation-by-failure, as failure of a process may be due to a lack of evidence. Vision and robotics systems often consist of a number of processes the majority of which involve numerical processing. In order to apply knowledge-based methods to such systems, a somewhat different approach to the traditional inference engine [50] may be required.

There have been several architectures composed for the representation of knowledge, including Scripts [197], Idealised Cognitive Models [137], and frames [160]. This book makes use of frames [160], which allow packaging of declarative knowledge with procedural knowledge, and have the ability to group facts, rules and processes into associative clusters [88]. These features are useful for problems in which much of the knowledge is in the form of procedural know-how or numerical processes, and where the facts, rules and processes can be partitioned in a way that is useful for the problem domain.

A *frame* is a data structure for representing a stereotyped situation. Information includes how to use the frame, what will occur next, and what to do if the expected does not occur. This forms a network of nodes and relations. Upper levels are fixed, representing information that is always true for a possible scenario. Lower levels consist of terminals, or slots, to be filled by specific data. The terminals can specify conditions which assignments must meet, and these assignments are usually smaller subframes. Once a frame is proposed for a situation, a matching process attempts to assign values to the terminals. Matching is controlled both by the frame, and the current system goals.

A frame system is a collection of related frames linked together.

Transformations between frames relate to important transitions in what is being represented. Links may be formed so that if a proposed frame cannot make correct terminal assignments, it can suggest other frames which may be appropriate for the given situation.

Frame terminals are normally filled with default assignments. These may be used for representing the most likely situations and general information. Defaults can be displaced by new items that better fit the current situation.

2.3.3   Pose determination

It is often desirable to find the orientation and position of an object relative to the robot. Tsai's camera calibration technique [224] is in common use. The technique computes computes camera external position and orientation relative to an object reference coordinate system, as well as the effective focal length, radial lens distortion, and image scanning parameters. Linnainmaa, Harwood, and Davis [145] and Lowe [146] determine object pose from a single image with six degrees of freedom (three in translation and three in rotation). Numerical solutions to pose determination are computationally intensive. However, for general robot navigation precise pose determination is often not required, and for ground-based robots, the object may have fewer degrees of freedom, thereby making a direct algebraic estimate practical.

2.4   Conclusion

This chapter presented research in vision-guided mobile robot systems. As well, the chapter included a review of computer vision techniques that are relevant to the methods presented in this book. This chapter highlighted a number of limitations in previous research in vision-guided mobile robots. Specifically:

- There has been little application of high-level vision techniques to mobile robots in the literature.

- The methods of high-level computer vision are unsuitable for application to robot navigation in their present form.

- No existing robot navigation systems are adequate to support moving reliably around a known object without some form of environmental map.

Chapter 3

Embodied Vision For Mobile Robots[1]

> *I suddenly see the solution of a puzzle-picture. Before there were branches there; now there is a human shape. My visual impression has changed and now I recognize that it has not only shape and colour but also a quite particular 'organization'.*

L. Wittgenstein [238]

Purposive, Animate Vision or Active Perception emphasises the relationship between perception and the perceiver's physiology, as well as that tasks performed must be considered in building intelligent visual systems [3]. However, such research generally considers low-level vision (e.g., segmentation, optical flow). There has been little consideration, to date, of the relationship between perception and the perceiver's physiology for high-level vision. This chapter discusses philosophical aspects of what is required to apply of high-level vision when the perceiver has a real body, i.e., an autonomous mobile robot. This chapter also proposes a framework of embodied categorisation for high-level vision and interaction for mobile robots. This framework is subsequently used throughout this book.

---

[1]Authors: Nick Barnes, Zhi-Qiang Liu, and Edwin Coleman

3.1   Introduction

The basic problem of autonomous robot navigation is to guide a robot
through an environment to a goal, and possibly interact with entities
in the environment. For an autonomous robot to be practical in most
applications, its movement must be largely continuous, and at a speed
that brings it to its intended goal quickly enough for the task. In an
indoor environment this may be a few cm/sec, or for outdoor vehicle guidance, up to 100 km/hour. For most applications, the robot's
view of the environment should be updated every few seconds, or even
fractions of a second.

Vision recovers more data from well-lit environments in comparison to range-based sensors. However, range-based sensors are more
frequently used for robot navigation. The key problem is that classical
computer vision methods are generally too slow. As such, successful
mobile robot systems almost invariably use non-classical methods that
are often highly adapted for a particular domain (e.g., road-following
systems [45]).

This chapter argues that concepts are necessary to facilitate the use
of high-level vision for robot guidance. Further, the conceptual framework implied by classical computer vision is not appropriate for this
task. The classical computer vision paradigm implicitly assumes that
things in the world are objectively subdivided into categories. A vision-
guided robot, however, is embodied, i.e., it has a physical presence in
the world. It follows from this embodiment that the robot generally
operates within a finite number of particular environments and is generally task-directed. The combination of operating in an environment
and on a task is sometimes referred to as *situatedness*. Embodiment
enables a conceptual system to be established that facilitates the use of
high-level vision for robot navigation. This chapter presents a method
for applying embodied categorisation or embodied concepts. Overall,
the book presents a robot navigation system based on these principles.
Other systems that successfully apply vision to guide robots in a manner that is consistent with these principles are also presented in this
chapter for completeness.

3.1.1   Embodiment

Embodiment, for humans, is the theory that abstract meaning, reason
and imagination have a bodily basis [123]. Embodiment is formed by

the nature of our bodies, including perception and motor movement, and of our physical and social interactions with the world.

Lakoff [137] considers categorisation to be the basic element of thought, perception, action and speech. To see something as a kind of thing involves categorisation. We reason about categories or kinds of things, and perform kinds of actions. The human conceptual system arises from conceptual embodiment, and is a product of our experience, both direct bodily experience, and indirect experience through social interaction.

If human thought, perception and action are based on categorisation, and this categorisation is embodied, then we should consider the proposition that embodied categorisation/embodied concepts may form a useful paradigm for robot perception.

3.1.2 Phenomena and noumena

Bennet [17] offers a analysis of Kant's [126] distinction between phenomena and noumena. The word phenomena covers all the things, processes and events that we can know about by means of senses. Statements about phenomena are equivalent to statements about sensory states, or the appearance of things. From these, Kant distinguishes noumena as anything that is not phenomenal, something which is not a sensory state, and cannot be the subject of sensory encounter. Noumena are sometimes equated with the 'things in themselves'.

For the argument of this chapter, the important distinction is that there are objects, processes, events, etc., which exist in the world, but as humans, we do not have access to objects themselves, but rather to sensory states pertaining to objects (naturally, sensory states also may not pertain to objects, such as hallucinations). This has strong implications for any research in computer vision. A computer vision system can never perceive everything about an object, as it does not have access to the object itself but only to its own sensory states. Similarly, a robot is restricted in what it can establish about an object by what it can experience of that object. A distinction between 'visible objects' and 'physical objects' has also been made in robotics [109].

3.2 The Classical Computer Vision Paradigm

The classical computer vision approach [155] begins with an image, which is transformed by segmentation into a primal sketch, and then

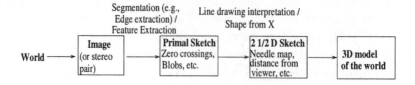

Figure 3.1: The classical model of computer vision.

composed into a 2 1/2 D sketch. From this, the system infers what objects are in the real world (Figure 3.1). The paradigm aims to "capture some aspect of reality by making a description of it using a symbol". It describes a sequence of representations that attempt to facilitate the "recovery of gradually more objective, physical properties about an object's shape." [155]

This approach assumes that the visible part of the real world can be described from a raw image. This is a general model that rejects any role for the system's embodiment or physiology: it must cater for all embodiments, all purposes, and all environments. As such, there must be either a single, uniquely correct categorisation for all the objects in the world, or vision must enumerate all possible descriptions and categories of the visible objects.

3.2.1   Non-classical computer vision

Active perception research emphasises the manipulation of visual parameters to acquire useful data about a scene [3]. For example, computation can be reduced by considering the context of behaviour, particularly by controlling the direction of gaze, which provides additional constraints, thereby simplifying early vision [10].

Model-based methods match sets of features, which are derived from an image, to candidate values or value ranges. A match suggests a particular structure or object is visible. In this way, the model specifies a description of an object in terms of features it can recognise. This interpretation of model-based representation does not assume there is a uniquely correct description for the visible part of the world.

However, model-based computer vision is often disembodied. For instance, the aspect graph, as discussed in Chapter 2, represents a series of generic views of an object. The views are geometrically derived, based on what can theoretically appear in an image. There is no consideration of what can actually be perceived, other than that features such as edges can, in general, be perceived. This often leads to redundant representation, and can result in millions of generic views being required to represent a complex object [76]. Matching may be a lengthy process, even if hierarchical indexing is used [33]. In computer vision this is referred to as the *indexing problem* [76]. In Artificial Intelligence the problem of determining what knowledge is relevant to a particular situation is called the *knowledge access problem* [61]. This problem can easily lead to excessive computation, so it is important to model-based vision systems which will guide robots.

While recent research has advanced significantly, some of the original problems of classical computer vision being a 'general' vision still appear in recent papers. For instance, Dickinson and Mextaxas [55] propose that the difficulties posed by fine structural detail for preprocessing an image may be overcome by abstracting "salient regions" from image detail. The relevant Macquarie dictionary definition of "salient" is "prominent or conspicuous" [1]. The fact that features are prominent and conspicuous does not imply that these are what a computer vision feature extraction method will find. Moreover, even if feature extraction does find a salient region, it does not mean that it will be relevant to the problem at hand. Greatly varying features of an object may be relevant for different purposes.

3.3 Problems with Classical Computer Vision

The classical framework has been the basis of considerable development in computer vision. However, there are limitations which are apparent in tasks that involve classification. High-level vision tasks, such as object recognition, rely on classification, as do many tasks that may be performed by vision in order to guide a robot. Here, classical computer vision faces some major problems, because there is no uniquely correct description of the world, and the list of possible descriptions is infinite for practical purposes.

Dupre [64] argues that there is no unique, natural categorisation. A general vision program must be able to uniquely classify all living organisms. However, Dupre details examples where scientific taxonomy and everyday language do not coincide. In fact they cross-classify organisms in complex ways that cannot be reconciled. Dupre shows that science does not have a uniquely correct method of classifying species.

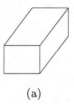

(a)

Figure 3.2: This line-drawing could be described as: (a) a glass cube; (b) an inverted open box; (c) a wire frame in a box shape; or, (d) three boards forming a solid angle.

The recognised classification methods have problems with hybridisation, evolution, and incomplete delineation. Note that this does not mean there is no good way of classifying biological organisms. Rather, there are many good methods of classification, sometimes equally good, and which one is most suitable depends on the purpose of the classification.

If there is no unique classification of living things, then clearly there is no unique classification of all things in the world. Further, other types of objects suffer from similar classification ambiguities. Enumeration of the almost infinite number of possible classifications of an object is intractable. Consider an image of 'a computer'. This may contain a monitor, which for some purposes will be a component of the computer, and for others it will not. Also, the monitor may be classified as a television, electronic components, or even a chair, etc.

If there is no unique classification of objects, and the number of possible classifications is very large, then computer vision cannot practically classify all the objects that may appear in a scene without consideration of the purpose of classification.

This raises the question of how objects should be categorised if there is no uniquely correct method. The philosophy of the mind gives a possible solution for vision-guided robots: this is embodied categories. *Objects should be classified by the way the robot relates to them.*

3.4 Applying Embodied Concepts in Human Vision

There is a distinction that can be drawn between *viewing* a scene, and *perceiving* something about the scene. Wittgenstein [238] uses the phrase *noticing an aspect* to describe the experience of noticing something about a scene for the first time, e.g., viewing a face and seeing (noticing) a likeness to another face. After noticing an aspect, the face does not change, but we see it differently. Noticing an aspect is not interpretation in a high-level sense as there is no conscious falsifiable hypothesis made at this stage, although it may be made subsequently. Consider Figure 3.2 from [238], and the descriptions (a) to (d): each provides a different suggestion of what the same diagram may be. By considering each one separately, we are able to *see* the diagram as one thing or another. This is not an interpretation about what the diagram represents. In seeing the diagram as an inverted open box we perceive the diagram in a particular way, but do not necessarily consciously hypothesise that it is as such, although we may do so subsequently.

There are two ways to view Figure 3.3. After seeing one aspect, a mental effort is needed to see the other. In seeing one aspect, we are not necessarily saying this object *is* a cube with the top line on the front face. In seeing something *as* something for the first time, the object appears to have changed, although what we look at is clearly unchanged. We may have noticed an organisation in what we see that suggests a structure of what is being looked at. For instance, we may determine that two lines previously considered to be separate are actually a single line. A way of understanding seeing-as is to consider what a group of lines or features may be a picture of. For instance, Figure 3.2 could be a picture of any of the things that are described in the captions.

Figure 3.3: The Necker cube. Is the top horizontal line or the bottom horizontal line actually on the front face of the cube?

This type of seeing is conceptual. Human vision does not simply provide a list of objects to which reason can apply concepts and draw interpretations. Perceptual mechanisms may apply at an early stage in the visual process, particularly in what is often considered early visual processing. Perceptual mechanisms may apply concepts before any interpretation begins.

3.4.1   Models play an analogous role in computer vision

Computer vision research that determines the 3D structure of an object based on line drawings is generally referred to as "interpretation of line drawings" [210]. Here, the word "interpretation" describes the process of applying constraints from geometry to the relations between the lines. In object recognition, interpretation is often a multi-staged process. For instance, initially interpreting what is an edge pixel and then what is an edge, subsequently the interpretation of the image as line-drawing, etc. Finally, a hypothesis may be made about the object category. It is well known that ambiguous drawings such as that in Figure 3.2 cause difficulties for such systems.

If a vision system extracted the set of edges that looked like Figure 3.2, a working hypothesis would be required as to whether the edges correspond to a box where the concavity is above or below the two larger surfaces. Further ambiguity would be added if the edges extracted were broken and the line drawing of Figure 3.2 were just one possible way of filling in the gaps. In this case, some form of model must be applied in order to draw out a sensible conclusion about the basic structure underlying what appears. Underlying the decision to extract edges is an implicit model that supposes that edges are a useful feature for the type of scene being examined.

After a model has been used to interpret the basic structure of an image there may be many possible interpretations that are consistent with the basic structure. For example, if we determine that the structure is the top and side surfaces of an enclosed box, then this box may be consistent with a battery charger or a shoe box. Other evidence, such as "we are in a shoe shop" may lead to the interpretation "it is a shoe box".

Thus, models can be usefully applied from the very earliest stage of computer vision, and are necessary, even if in implicit form, to see an array of intensity values as portraying a particular underlying structure. *Conceptual intervention may be necessary at the earliest stages of computer vision.*

Vision for robots

Categorisation is necessary for vision systems in order to give descriptions that are adequate to guide a robot through a non-trivial environment. Simple categories like 'free-space' and 'obstacle' may be sufficient in some cases. Brooks [28] noted that a robot has its own perceptual world that is different from other robots and humans. The perceptual world is defined by the robot's embodiment. Robots may need categories that are different from human categories to deal with their sensory world, which arises out of their specific embodiment. These are embodied categories.

3.5 Embodiment of Vision-guided Robots

Brooks [30] considers the key idea of embodiment is to ground regress of abstract symbols. Being grounded is essential for real-world interaction, but a robot's embodiment also constrains the relationships it will have with objects and the environment. There are many possible categories and features that may be used in a robot vision model. Categories and features that are relevant to the robot can be selected using the constraints of the robot's embodiment.

A vision-guided mobile robot acts upon the world in a causal manner, and is able to perceive the results of its actions. It is embodied in the sense that it has a particular physical existence in the world which constrains its interaction and perception. These constraints include:

1. Robot movement is constrained by its physical bulk. A particular robot's structure restricts its ability to fit into places, its ability to bring its sensors close to objects, and constrains the operations it may perform.

2. Robot movement is constrained by kinematics and a movement control system. Although some robots are omni-directional, many have finite turning circles, and are only able to move in certain ways. In cluttered environments this leads to the *piano movers problem*.

3. The types of surfaces and environments a robot can traverse is restricted. Many robots, due to lack of ground clearance, structural robustness, or motor strength, are restricted to indoor operations. For outdoor robots, much of the earth's surface is not

traversable by wheeled vehicles. As well, legged robots can travel on a greater range of surfaces, but have other limitations. Further, some indoor robots may have difficulties with rough floor surfaces, inclines, and stairs.

4. Most robots travel on the ground, and hence will never perceive objects from some viewpoints, or act upon them from certain angles. Also, depending a robot's size, obstacles taller than a particular height will be problematic, while smaller obstacles can sometimes be ignored. Similarly, objects such as overhead shelves do not obstruct robots which are shorter than them.

5. Robot perception is constrained by sensor limitations. For instance, cameras require sufficient light (e.g., visible, infra-red), and contrast to distinguish an edge between two objects. Digital cameras only perceive features at a particular scale. Features smaller than one pixel are indiscernible, while objects larger than the pixel array cannot be perceived from a single viewpoint. The effect of camera resolution on scale depends on the robot-to-object distance and camera zoom. Further, odometry always has errors, so position is seldom precise.

6. A robot is also embodied in its software. A vision-guided robot that works only on the basis of image edges will be unable to distinguish objects that have identical wire frames. As well, the objects may be different colours, have different surface albedo, or have surfaces of different shapes or texture.

3.5.1   Embodiment, task and environment

Dreyfus argues that context is crucial to the way human intelligence handles the knowledge access problem. A global anticipation is required which is characteristic of our embodiment [61]. Searle [200] describes this as the background. The background is the enormous collection of common-sense knowledge, ways of doing things, etc., that are required for us to perform basic tasks. The background cannot be made explicit as there is no limit to the number of additions that would have to be made to prevent possible misinterpretations, and each addition would, in turn, be subject to interpretation.

With respect to different backgrounds, any visual scene has an almost infinite number of true descriptions. A photograph of a house may be equally well described as 'my home', 'Uncle Bill's house', 'a charming Californian bungalow', 'an obstacle', etc. A real-estate agent may use the 'charming' description, while a mobile robot may regard the house as an obstacle that is blocking the path to its required destination.

The fact that the robot has physical embodiment means that it has an associated context, which incorporates purpose (task), environment (spatial context), and naturally, a temporal context.

3.5.2 The role of the task

Situation theory can be seen as anchoring parameters, such as how entities are categorised in the situation in which they occur [237]. In robotics research, the term 'situated' has often been used in the sense that entities in the world can be seen by a robot in terms of their relationship with the robot [30]. For example, in the system of Horswill and Brooks [109], objects are classified as "the-object-I-am-tracking" or "everything-else" rather than having a category that has meaning beyond the robot's interaction. In terms of conceptual embodiment, the task defines a particular perspective and helps designate the facts that are relevant and those that can be ignored.

3.5.3 The role of the environment

The simple categorisation of Horswill and Brooks' system is adequate for the environment it inhabits, but maybe inadequate in others. The environment constrains a robot's possible experiences of the world, the possible events that can occur, and the scenes and objects that may appear. Even humans recognise objects more quickly and accurately in their typical contexts than when viewed in an unusual context (e.g., fire-hydrant in a kitchen) [19]. The most appropriate conceptual model varies with the environment.

3.6 Embodiment for Vision-guided Robots

The remaining sections present examples where embodiment principles have been applied to vision-guided robots. The focus is on classification and perception, and not reason and learning. These sections consider how a robot with a specific structure can perform effectively in the context of an environment and task. The aim is to show how the form

and content of a model-based conceptual framework can be constructed
to take advantage of a robot's embodiment. This demonstrates how
embodied concepts can be used in the construction of vision-guided
robots. Principles of embodied conceptualisation have been applied
to construct the vision-guided robot system that is presented in this
book. Further, other systems in the literature that implicitly apply
these principles are highlighted.

3.6.1   Physical embodiment

Chapter 4 describes how an embodied approach has been used to re-
define traditional viewer-centred representations. The embodied approach also gains specific computational and recognition advantages
for a robot. The embodiment of a robot allows model-based representations to be simplified, and hence made more practical.

The *scale problem* of which scale features should be modelled is
problematic when features are geometrically derived from a 3D model.
However, model views and features may be composed based on how
the object is perceived in images that are taken across the range of
distances at which the robot is to interact. In this case, the scale will
be effectively defined.

Edges that lack adequate contrast for detection should not be modelled. Further, as a robot's embodiment constrains which views of an
object it can see, views such as a car's underside may be removed from
the model, which yield computational and storage advantages.

A robot can gain perceptual advantages by utilising the way it
interacts. Robots move *causally* around objects. A robot does not
have to fully recognise an object from a single viewpoint that may
appear similar to other objects, or be partially occluded. A robot can
recognise the object by moving around it to find an unnoccluded view
and combining that with what was seen at the first surface. Chapter 8
demonstrates an experiment where two separate views of an object
appear identical. The robot is able to differentiate the views by knowing
which views appeared at previous known locations.

Embodied concepts can aid low-level vision tasks. Chapter 6 illustrates a system that combines knowledge about the basic structure
of an object with knowledge gained from edge matching. This knowledge is applied in order to add constraints and simplify tasks in shape-
from-shading, making tasks solvable that would previously have been
difficult. Also, computation time advantages can be gained through

task domain knowledge. In Chapter 5, candidate edges are only extracted within the range of candidate orientations that are possible for a match, given that a particular view of the object is visible, and that the restricted motion of the object relative to the robot. Extracting edges within restricted ranges of orientation is also discussed in [125].

Active perception methods often employ embodied mechanisms. For example, in *divergent stereo*, robots navigate down corridors with visually textured walls by equalising the optical flow in a pair of cameras which point toward either wall [192]. The actual appearance of optical flow in this type of situation is different for particular robots. For specific tasks, robots can employ direct mechanisms such as divergent stereo, where the environment supports them.

3.6.2 Embodiment in a task

The robot's task can partially define categorisation of objects. In Figure 3.5, an identical house may either be an obstacle, or 'Uncle Bill's House' depending on the task. Figure 3.6 shows a more complex example where the task defines what is an object of interest, and what can be seen as "everything-else". The task also defines which objects are potential obstacles. If an object blocks the path that the robot must take to complete the task, then it can be considered to be an obstacle. Whether or not it is a true obstacle is also determined by the robot's physical structure, as discussed in [27], (see Chapter 2).

It is not only the basic classification of an object that can be derived from the task. In Chapter 4, the object model is structured in terms of the relationship that the robot has with the object through the task. If the task is to identify an object, navigate around it, and dock at a particular location, then the robot is not generally required to perceive the object from a particularly close range. Thus, the robot's object model does not incorporate views which appear close to the object, except possibly at the docking surface. Also, the combination of robot-to-object distance and finite resolution of its cameras dictate what scale of features the robot cannot perceive. The robot does not have to entirely differentiate the object from a single frame, but can move and accumulate evidence from several viewpoints. Thus, its model can be simplified for each view without degrading recognition performance.

Further, spatial concepts such as 'nearness', depend on the scale of the entities [47]. How close the robot should be to the object in Chapter 4 is dependent not only on the robot and object scale, but

also on the task. For instance, the instruction 'move around the other
side of the object' may not require the robot to move as close as would
'dock with the object'.

3.6.3   Embodiment in an environment

The environment affects the way a mobile robot should behave and perceive. In Figure 3.4, the robot may require a bold exploration approach
to find its way around an uncluttered safe static indoor environment.
The robot may assume that if it does not have enough information to
know where it is, then it should move around to explore. However, the
robot may need to move cautiously in the outdoor environment with
fast moving dangerous objects such as cars, gutters and puddles, with
premature exploratory movements possibly being destructive. Other
aspects of the environment will also have an influence on both behaviours, and perception strategies or models. For instance, robots
that operate in difficult visual conditions (e.g., dull light) require perceptual models to be optimised for what can be seen. In Chapter 4 it is
proposed that only features that can be detected consistently by sensors
in the required environment should be used to identify the object.[1]

The visual nature of the environment may constrain models. In uncluttered environments, the required models may be different to those
used in environments with a high density of visual features (e.g., a
forest). Some of the systems for obstacle detection and localisation
discussed in Chapter 2 implicitly make use of an environment model
by making strong assumptions about the environment in which the
robot operates. Further, offices can often be represented as consisting
of smooth walls and floors which join at a sharp juncture. In these
environments, discontinuities of objects and doors generally appear as
vertical lines. This structure was used to advantage in the system of
Braunegg [23]. Aggarwal [214] uses the natural constraints of an outdoor environment. In a system based in the Rocky mountains, visual
localisation can be performed based on the visible shape of the horizon.
Also, in outdoor urban environments the model size can be contained
by considering only a restricted set of features that are adequate in
that environment [215].

---

[1]Some exceptions may be appropriate. For example, there may be a particular
feature, such as a label, that is unique and allows fast and easy recognition of the
object If this feature is only visible under certain lighting conditions, it may still be
desirable to keep the feature in the model to resolve ambiguity for the special case.

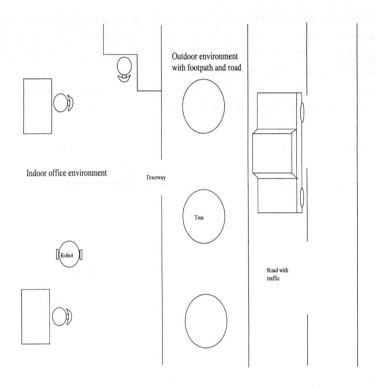

Figure 3.4: Different environments require different models and different behaviour. A robot moving in a static office may roam freely, whereas such behaviour may be dangerous outdoors near a busy road. Also, the lighting and types of structures seen indoors may be different from those outdoors.

Although a robot needs to take the environment into account it does not mean that a system must be restricted to a single environment. It is easy to imagine a mechanism for recognising a change of environment, such as moving through the door of Figure 3.4 into the outdoor world. Such a mechanism could trigger a transition for the robot to use a different perceptual model, different behaviours, and perhaps even different sensors.

3.7 Conclusion

A physically embodied robot is present in an environment, and typically engaged in tasks. The physical embodiment of a robot, and its tasks and environment constrains the relationship the robot has with entities in the world. Specifically, it constrains how the robot can perceive and interact with other entities. These constraints can be used as the basis for robot classification and object models. The construction of classification and models based on embodiment is referred to here as conceptual embodiment. As discussed, classical computer vision is inadequate for guiding mobile robots. By the application of conceptual embodiment, high-level model-based vision techniques can be made effective for robot guidance. The robotic system presented in this book has been constructed based on conceptual embodiment.

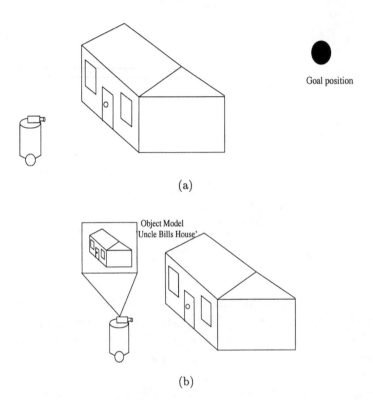

Figure 3.5: The task may mean that the robot has totally different categorisations for the same view of the same object. (a) Task: move to the goal position. Description: the robot is currently viewing an obstacle. (b) Task: Find 'Uncle Bill's house'. Description: The robot correctly identifies 'Uncle Bill's house'.

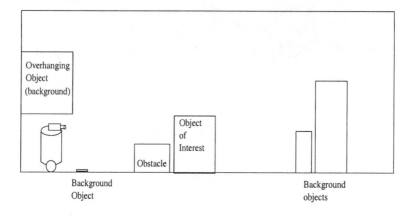

Figure 3.6: The object of interest is defined by the task. Whether an object is an obstacle, or a background object may also be partially defined by the task, and partially by the physical structure of the robot. The large objects behind the object of interest are not obstacles because they are not close to the required path of the robot. The very small object in front of the robot is not an obstacle because the physical structure of the robot allows it to ignore such objects. The obstacle very near the object of interest blocks the required path and is significant in view of the robot's physical structure.

Chapter 4

Object Recognition Mobile Robot Guidance

If it is to interact intelligently and effectively with its environment, a robot must recognize and locate objects in that environment.
W. E. L. Grimson [89]

Having presented an embodied vision approach to visually-guided robot navigation, this chapter discusses putting it into practice. The ability to uniquely identify and locate objects in its environment enables a robot to differentiate similar objects in order to interact with a specified object. This chapter describes a method for object recognition and navigation that is designed specifically for robot interaction. It is based on canonical-views, a novel object representation which realises principles of embodied vision. This chapter also presents a direct algebraic method for finding the orientation and position of the specified object.

4.1 Introduction

Mobile robot guidance systems generally focus on the problem of navigating through an environment, often by localising with respect to the environment, and moving according to a global map, (e.g., [43, 143, 212]). Objects are usually treated as obstacles to be avoided. Few systems in the literature examine the problem of recognising and interacting with objects. However, many tasks that mobile robots may perform (e.g., in dangerous environments, manufacturing, mining, and agricultural applications) involve identifying specific objects and performing predetermined interactions with them. In this chapter, a model-based object recognition system is described that uniquely identifies a specified object, and enables an autonomous mobile robot to move with respect to the object, and interact or dock without collision.

This chapter introduces an active approach to recognition, which emphasises the *causal* nature of interaction, particularly, changes in a robot's perception of a stationary object are caused by robot actions. The system is able to focus its attention on the object with which it is required to interact. Other visible features are regarded as background, and non-target objects are possible obstacles. The vision system's purpose is to facilitate the task of robot navigation. Hence, a task-directed approach is taken by using the constraints of robot navigation to help make vision processing efficient. In order to facilitate this efficiency, a novel representation called *canonical-views* is introduced. Canonical-views are an active, viewer-centred object model, specifically designed for robot navigation. Canonical-views are optimised to represent what the robot can see in practice, rather than what theoretically appears.

There are two stages at which object recognition is used in the system: initially recognise the object when it is first seen; and to check the robot's relative position as it navigates around the object.[1] In the second stage, the canonical-view model predicts which view will appear next based on the view last recognised and the movements performed. Further, consider that the object to be recognised by the robot is defined by the task, so in general, the system has only to match a single view of the object. The system does not require an environment map as it navigates with a focus on the specified object, and detects and avoids obstacles as it moves.

In contrast to the system of Vaughn and Arkin [229], the system presented does not require a transformation of its model, *a priori* constraints, or initial estimates of the relative location of the object. Further, in the system presented the robot may approach the object from any angle.

Object recognition systems such as that by Dickinson *et al.* [54], are restricted to objects composed of distinct volumetric parts. The system presented has no such restriction. Further, systems that emphasise indexing are advantageous for *unexpected object recognition*, but offer

---

[1]These are parallel to the drop-off and update problem for localisation.

less computational benefits when the task is to identify a particular object, i.e., *expected object recognition.*

4.2 System Perspective

Object recognition comprises one part of the vision-guided robot navigation system. Its place in the overall system architecture is shown in Figure 4.1. The architecture for object recognition can be seen in Figure 4.2. The system interfaces to image pre-processing, as described in Chapter 5, by requesting candidate image edges based on a particular range of angle and curvature. It attempts to match the candidate image edges to model edges based on simple relative spatial features. Once a match is found, the system determines the orientation of the object and its distance, relative to the robot. The match may then be verified by testing surface shape, as discussed in the next chapter. After a match is confirmed, navigation will proceed, as discussed in Chapter 7.

Assuming the robot is close enough, the system is able to recognise a 3D object regardless of pose. The match finds image-to-model correspondences which are used to calculate the four degree of freedom inverse perspective transform which gives approximate object orientation and position.

4.3 Object Recognition

4.3.1 Canonical-views

The system recognises both the object and the view through the use of a viewer-centred, model-based recognition technique, called Canonical-views, which is a representation scheme specialised for robot navigation. Although, in general, viewer-centred representations are not very useful in real applications, canonical-views overcome key problems that inhibit their application to robot navigation by taking a conceptual embodiment approach. As discussed in Chapter 2, aspect graphs may redundantly represent one surface in many views which are differentiated only by visual events that are not observable in practice, and there is no adequate view indexing mechanism [76]. Canonical-views take advantage of the constraints imposed on recognition of robot navigation, and have been designed to resolve the above problems for robot

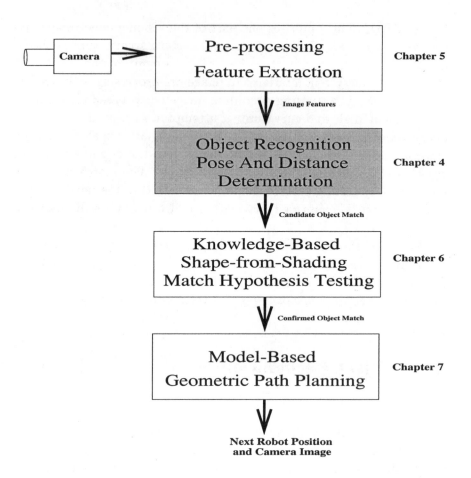

Figure 4.1: This chapter describes the object recognition and pose determination part of the system architecture.

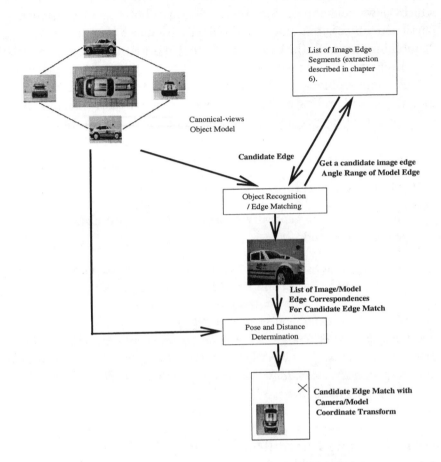

Figure 4.2: The architecture for the canonical-view matching system. It interfaces to edge extraction, as described in Chapter 6, by requesting an edge with orientation within a particular range. It presents a candidate view match with pose and position for verification of shape, as described in Chapter 5, then for use for navigation, as shown in Chapter 6.

vision, but maintain the advantage of a fast 2D-to-2D match.

Ground-based robots have a characteristic perspective of objects which defines the scale at which object views can be perceived, and which views can appear. Further, when a robot has to deal with a particular object, the indexing problem is reduced to a single object. Combining this with the causality of robot motion, the robot generally only needs to match a single view. Clearly, there is an exception for the drop-off problem, where the robot encounters the object for the first time, with no estimate of the view it is currently facing. The canonical-view representation also considers the following issues:

1. Real cameras are not point but have finite size;

2. Objects have features that contribute little to recognition;

3. Robots are not generally expected to recognise objects at very close range; and,

4. Camera images are discrete, thus for a particular viewing range, features below a certain size are not distinguishable.

Definition 1 *A* canonical-view *is a set of neighbouring characteristic views which: are differentiated only by visual events involving features of size s for which $\frac{s}{b} \leq k$, where b is the size of the largest surface in the view, and k is constant; and only models features that contribute significantly to recognition.*

Small features, such as car wheel-nuts, may generate many visual events (see Figure 4.4(a)). However, there is little value in distinguishing such views for a robot moving at some distance from where some of the views may not be visible, and others are so close together that they are unimportant given the comparatively course scale of mobile robot motion. Clearly, the selection of the parameter k is dependent on embodied variables, which include: the minimum number of pixels that a feature needs to have in order to be detected by the system; image resolution and the portion of the image the object is expected to occupy given the anticipated maximum distance; and, the camera focal length.

Further, the edges extracted from the wheel nuts are poor due to low contrast (see Figure 4.4(b)). Also, consider the case where small circles approximately the size of the wheel nuts appear on wall-paper behind

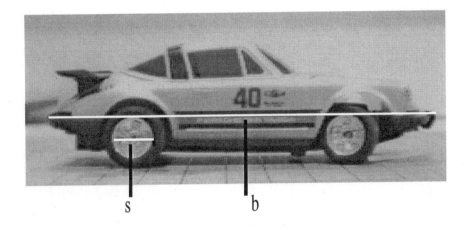

Figure 4.3: Setting a value for k: l is the width of the side of the car, k is set empirically to allow s to be up to the size of the wheel.

(a)

(b)

Figure 4.4: Edges extracted from the wheel nuts are unclear and inconsistent due to poor contrast, and thus make poor features.

the robot. Here such a feature would contribute little to differentiating the object from its background. Thus, a canonical-view may exclude: features that are common in the environment; features likely to cause inconsistent edge segmentation; and, surface texture.

Views where the features are a subset of another view may be excluded in order to reduce the number of model views. For example, an aspect graph for three neighbouring faces of a cube (as shown in Figure 4.5) would have seven views. A possible canonical-view representation would have nodes for views one, three and five. Images with more than one surface visible could match with any of the corresponding canonical-views. Note also that all views are a subset of view seven so a valid canonical-view representation could consist only of view seven. In this case, a match with any of the component surfaces should return a true match. To model this way would require disjunctions across views in view matching.

Definition 2 *A* canonical-view representation *represents only canonical views of an object that are not a subset of the surfaces modelled for any other view, and defines a link between all views that are neighbouring in the robot's path.*

The system initially must check the image against every view in the model to find the best match, as object pose is entirely unknown. However, once the first match is made and a move performed, the next view is *causally* defined by the previous position and the movement. By combining the robot's previous estimate of its position and orientation with the odometric measure of the move performed, the system can predict which view the system will expect to see. Thus, the system generally needs to match only one view for each move. Further the system can discriminate between object surfaces which are almost identical on the basis of temporal information about previous views. Through linking of neighbouring views, the representation is indexed by the robot path around the object. Thus, canonical-views instantiate the causal relationship between object views defined by the robot navigation problem described here.

For a traditional computer vision system, protrusions out of an object, and holes in an object generally must be modelled from all theoretically possible view points. Thus, views should be included for any viewing points within the convex hull of the object. Holes and protrusions may be treated differently in robot vision. If the robot is larger than the object or of a similar scale, it will typically not be in a position to identify the object from a close proximity to holes or protrusions. Thus, holes and protrusions can be treated as standard surface features, and may lead to additional views if they appear large enough from the viewing distances expected. However, if the object is comparatively large and has large holes or protrusions, the robot may be expected to move within the object's convex hull. In this case, the model should include additional views based on images from such positions.

Figure 4.6 shows a model car used in some of our navigation experiments. Each of the four views shown represent the adjacent surface of

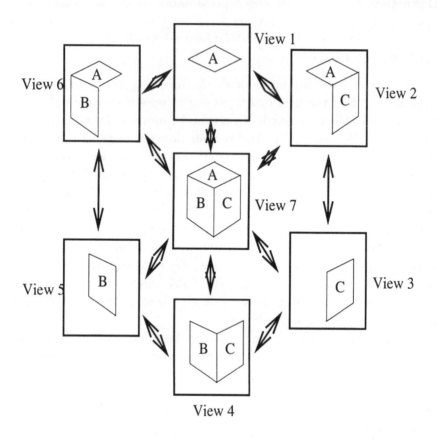

Figure 4.5: A partial aspect graph representation of a cube. Views 1-6 all consist only of subsets of the surfaces appearing in view 7.

the car. The canonical views generated overlap at the corners. Model
feature value ranges in the experiments were derived manually from
segmented edge images of the views, including images from extreme
ends of modelled view visibility. It is important to consider what the
robot can actually perceive, rather than geometric derivation from a
CAD model in order to derive practical models for robot navigation.

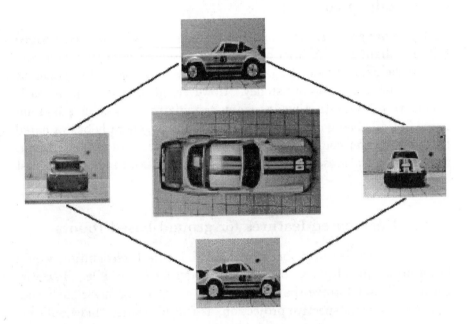

Figure 4.6: The four canonical views of a model car. Each view represents the adjacent surface of the car. The views overlap at the car's
corners so that small odometry/pose errors will not lead to incorrect
view estimation.

4.3.2 Match verification

Edge-based matching can differentiate many classes of objects. Causal
matching of more than one view ensures that the system is able to
discriminate between objects where segmentation errors may have lead
to an improper match, and where objects may have one or more identical surfaces. However, there may be some objects that have identical
wire-frames. Such objects may confuse an edge-match based system
despite the fact that the objects are clearly distinguishable based on

surface shape. Consider that edges extracted from an image taken from any particular view around one of the objects could be identical to the edges extracted for the other object from the same relative view point. In this case, shape-from-shading can be used to verify the identification of surfaces based on knowledge of the shape, as shown in Chapter 6.

4.3.3   Edge matching

View matching is performed as a multi-stage process which is described fully in Chapter 5. A brief overview is presented here to give a context to the next section. Edge match quality is evaluated by geometric verification and pose consistency. However, geometric verification is expensive to evaluate, thus, as many candidates as possible are eliminated initially based on spatial relations that can generally be evaluated by direct integer comparison. Unary edge features are evaluated first, then binary features are matched to the model forming a depth-first search.

4.3.4   Edge-based features for ground-based robots

Ideally, surface features for viewer-centred object recognition would be invariant for all views over which the surface is visible. However, Burns *et al.*, [34] prove that there are no general-case invariant visual features under perspective projection, as feature values "blow out" for some views, see Figure 4.7(a). However, some features exhibit *low view variation*, where the variation is small in extent over a large fraction of the views. In Figure 4.7(a), although the features of surface one have extreme values, recognition is still possible based on surfaces two and three. In the case of objects with adjoining surfaces at acute angles, (see Figures 4.7(b) and (c)). the features of all visible surfaces may be in extreme ranges. Such objects are difficult for viewer-centred object recognition.

The model uses features that are similar to those in [34]:

1. edge orientation (Continuous range);

2. intersecting end-points of edges ([True, False]); and

3. relative edge location ([Above, Above1, Below, Below1, Collinear] and [Left-of, Left-of1 Right-of, Right-of1]).

Note that the features discussed in this section are specifically for ground-based mobile robots, where the motion of the robot is restricted to the ground plane, as shown in Figure 4.8. By considering features for the case where the motion is restricted by robot embodiment specifically, rather than using an analysis for unrestricted views such as in [89] leads to more efficient matching.

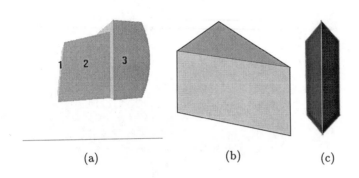

(a)   (b)   (c)

Figure 4.7: Examples of feature "blow out". (a) The features of surface one, the back of a computer terminal, are at extreme values, while surface two and three are normal. (b) A wedge shaped object. (c) View from the tip of the wedge, all visible surfaces are distorted. Such objects are difficult for viewer-centred object recognition.

Edge orientation, η, relative to the image y-axis is used as there is only rotation about the Z axis, as shown in Figure 4.8. Perspective variance of η is proportional to the angle, α, of the edge to the image plane, and the relative displacement, Δd, of the line end-points from the camera focal centre. Also, as α increases, foreshortening the horizontal component of the edge, η may decrease. Edge orientation ranges can be estimated using Equation (4.4) from the next section at the extreme points of the required view visibility.

Relative edge location is a useful feature due to restricted robot motion. An edge pair is labelled above/below/left-of/right-of if every point on one edge is above/below/left-of/right-of every point of the other, for every viewing angle. If at least one point on one edge is above/below/left-of/right-of every point on the other, for every viewing angle, then the edge is labelled above1/below1/left-of1/right-of1. An edge pair is labelled collinear if the difference between the gradients and

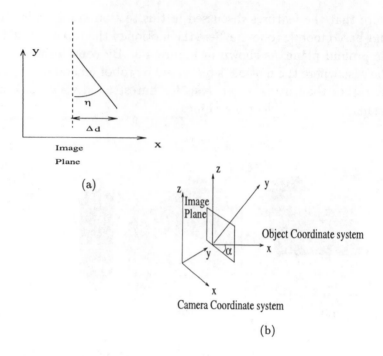

Figure 4.8: (a) An edge as it appears in the image plane. (b) The camera to object transform.

y-intercepts of the edges in absolute image coordinates are less than threshold values. If a pair of edges has a left-of or right-of relation at one point of view space, it will be true whenever both edges are visible, except when one edge is on a limb which is above or below the surface of the other edge, see Figure 4.9. Above/Below relations are affected by perspective. Parallel lines, coplanar in Z, will not cross, but, non-parallel edges, or edges at varying depths may cross, (see Figure 4.10). Perspective effects vary with displacement from the image centre in x, and with α. The relations above1/below1/left-of1/right-of1 are for co-terminating edges, for example, edges that meet at a right angle.

A special case for these relations is included for collinear edges. If edges are collinear, and their termination points are close, the edge extraction method used may incorrectly form them into a single line. To handle this case, a single image edge may be matched to multiple image edges as long as all relations for both edges are satisfied. In this case, above1/below1/left-of1/right-of1 will be true if both edges actually correspond to the same edge.

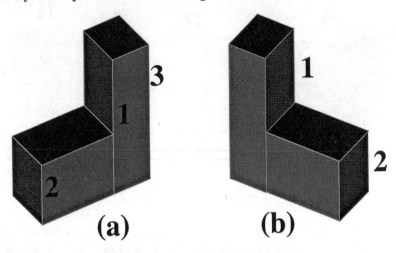

Figure 4.9: In (a) edge 1 is right-of edge 2, while in (b) edge 1 is left-of edge 2, but edge 1 is left-of edge 3 whenever both are visible.

Feature ranges are estimated by considering perspective projection for views which maximise variation. This can be empirically found from images at extreme views, or estimated using the perspective equations for rotation only about the Z-axis, see Equations 4.1 and 4.2.

The result of a successful match is an indication of the view matched, and correspondence between edge end-points in the image and the model.

4.3.5 View prediction

The constant distance from where the robot views an object is large compared to the size of the object. The change of views as a robot moves around the object can be predicted directly from the orientation of the camera with respect to the object. This was the case for all objects used in the experiments of this book. For large objects, or views where the robot's distance from the object will vary (e.g., a docking surface), the robot's relative position would also need to be taken into account.

Let η be the current orientation of the robot's camera with respect to absolute object coordinates when the last image of the object was taken, and let $\delta\eta$ be the change in the camera orientation since. Thus,

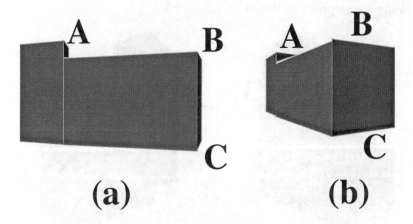

Figure 4.10: Edge B and C are parallel and at the same depth. However, edge A is at a different depth: (a) A is above B, B is above C, (b) B is above C, but A is not above B.

the predicted relative orientation of the camera to the object in object coordinates is $\eta + \delta\eta$. Each canonical-view has a continuous range of possible viewing locations. These ranges are stored in the model in absolute model coordinates. The ranges overlap a little between views. For a given approximate distance from the object, the range of locations can be specified by the orientation the observing camera must have in order to include this view.[2] The view of the object to be recognised can thus be evaluated directly by comparing it against the view ranges. See Figure 4.11.

4.4   Determining Object Pose and Distance

Six degree of freedom numerical pose determination is not required as the robot moves on the ground, and camera elevation can be varied without calibration. There are four degrees of freedom (one rotational and three translational) for calculating the respective locations of the robot and object. Further, general robot navigation does not require precise pose, hence a fast algebraic estimate can be used. An earlier attempt [11] at this problem assumed calibration of the camera height,

---

[2]If the object is small in the total field of view of the camera there is some variance in this depending on the angle subtended by the camera image.

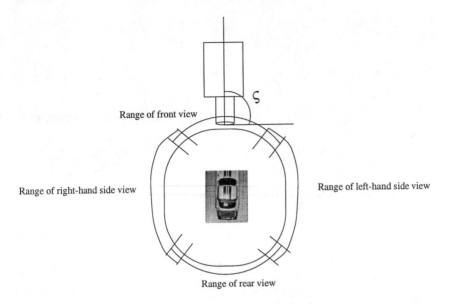

Range of front view

Range of right-hand side view

Range of left-hand side view

Range of rear view

Figure 4.11: The view currently to be recognised can be predicted directly from relative camera orientation. The overlapping ranges of orientations for each view are shown.

but this was found to be sensitive to camera tilt and ground plane irregularities in practice.

Figure 4.12 shows the model / camera coordinate transform. By inspection, the pin-hole camera perspective equations for image coordinates u and v are:

$$u = \frac{f(T_x + Y_m \cos\theta - X_m \sin\theta)}{T_y - Y_m \sin\theta - X_m \cos\theta}, \qquad (4.1)$$

$$v = \frac{f(Z_m + T_z)}{T_y - Y_m \sin\theta - X_m \cos\theta}, \qquad (4.2)$$

where X_m, Y_m, Z_m are the model coordinates, and T_x, T_y, T_z are the translations along the camera x, y and z axes of the model coordinate system.

Dividing (4.2) by (4.1) gives:

$$\frac{v}{u} = \frac{Z_m + T_z}{T_x + Y_m \cos\theta - X_m \sin\theta}. \qquad (4.3)$$

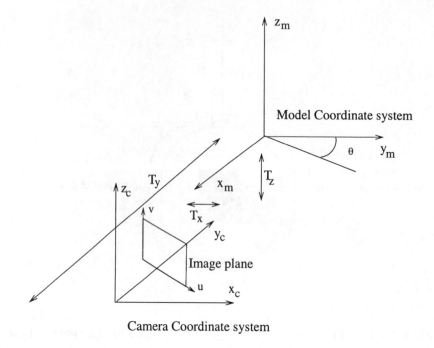

Figure 4.12: The transformation from the model to the camera coordinate systems.

The translations (T_x, T_y, T_z) may be eliminated from these equations by, considering edge segments in the image, rather than points:

$$\frac{\Delta v}{\Delta u} = \frac{\Delta Z_m}{\Delta Y_m \cos\theta - \Delta X_m \sin\theta}, \qquad (4.4)$$

where $\Delta u = u_2 - u_1$, $\Delta v = v_2 - v_1$, $\Delta X_m = X_{m2} - X_{m1}$, $\Delta Y_m = Y_{m2} - Y_{m1}$, and $\Delta Z_m = Z_{m2} - Z_{m1}$, and (u_1, v_1) and (u_2, v_2) are two points in the image, and (X_{m1}, Y_{m1}, Z_{m1}) and (X_{m2}, Y_{m2}, Z_{m2}) are corresponding model coordinates.

Now, consider the identities:

$$\sin(a - b) = \sin a \cos b - \sin b \cos a, \qquad (4.5)$$
$$\cos(a + b) = \cos a \cos b - \sin b \sin a. \qquad (4.6)$$

Also, let

$$(\sqrt{X^2 + Y^2}) \sin a = X, \tag{4.7}$$
$$(\sqrt{X^2 + Y^2}) \cos a = Y. \tag{4.8}$$

Substituting (4.7) and (4.8) into Equation (4.5), produces:

$$(\sqrt{X^2 + Y^2}) \sin(a - b) = X \cos b - Y \sin b, \tag{4.9}$$

Alternatively, let

$$(\sqrt{X^2 + Y^2}) \sin a = Y, \tag{4.10}$$
$$(\sqrt{X^2 + Y^2}) \cos a = X. \tag{4.11}$$

Substituting (4.10) and (4.11) into Equation (4.6), gives:

$$(\sqrt{X^2 + Y^2}) \cos(a + b) = Y \cos b - X \sin a. \tag{4.12}$$

An equation may now be deduced for θ, substituting (4.9) into (4.4), gives

$$\sin(\theta - \alpha) = \frac{\Delta Z_m \Delta u}{\Delta v \sqrt{\Delta X_m^2 + \Delta Y_m^2}}, \tag{4.13}$$

where $\tan \alpha = \frac{\Delta Y_m}{\Delta X_m}$.

Alternatively, substituting (4.12) into 4.4, gives

$$\cos(\theta + \alpha) = \frac{\Delta Z_m \Delta u}{\Delta v \sqrt{\Delta X_m^2 + \Delta Y_m^2}}, \tag{4.14}$$

where $\tan a = \frac{\Delta X_m}{\Delta Y_m}$.

(4.15) is derived by considering (4.2) for the vertical component of an edge, where $\overline{X}_m = (X_{m1} + X_{m2})/2$, and $\overline{Y}_m = (Y_{m1} + Y_{m2})/2$ are the mean model coordinates of the edge, and $\overline{T}_y = (T_{y1} + T_{y2})/2$ is the mean of the translations in Y to model points (X_{m1}, Y_{m1}, Z_{m1}) and (X_{m2}, Y_{m2}, Z_{m2}). Finally, consider (4.1) for the displacement of the vertical edge used in (4.15) from the image centre, where $\overline{T}_x = (T_{x1} + T_{x2})/2$ is the mean displacement of the model points.

$$\overline{T}_y = \frac{f \Delta Z_m}{\Delta v} + \overline{Y}_m \sin \theta + \overline{X}_m \cos \theta, \tag{4.15}$$
$$\overline{T}_x = -u \frac{\overline{T}_y - \overline{Y}_m \sin \theta - \overline{X}_m \cos \theta}{f} + \overline{Y}_m \cos \theta - \overline{X}_m \sin \theta. \tag{4.16}$$

Note that this derivation assumes no tilt in the camera angle. It could easily be modified to include this if required, provided that the tilt angle is known.

In practice, Equation 4.13 and 4.14 are used by taking the average of two displacements in u and v using four correspondence points in the image (4.14) gives only the magnitude of θ. For each view, the ideal points to use as a basis for pose determination are encoded into the model. These could be automatically determined using a heuristic search.

4.4.1 Active determination of the sign of θ

In the perspective projection case, the sign may be determined by finding the closer of two edges based on relative ratios of image to model displacement in v.

However, given orthographic projection, the sign may be determined from consecutive pose estimates. Figure 4.13, shows two consecutive views taken of an object. Let, the camera pan angle at the first position be ς_1, and ς_2 at the second position, and let $\Delta\varsigma = \varsigma_2 - \varsigma_1$. Also, let θ_1 be the estimate of the angle of an object surface to the camera axis at the first position, and θ_2 at the second. The signs of the angles θ_1 and θ_2 are unknown initially. Let $\phi_1 = \theta_1 + \Delta\varsigma$ be the estimate of the new angle if $\theta_1 \geq 0$, and let $\phi_2 = \theta_1 + \Delta\varsigma$ be the estimate of the new angle if $\theta_1 < 0$. The estimate ϕ_i with the closest absolute value to the new system estimate θ_2 can be taken to be the more correct estimate, and so its sign is used as the sign of θ_2. Note that as the relative angles between all the object's visible surfaces are known, it is trivial to calculate the angle if only one of the object's other surfaces is visible in the second image.

Once an estimate of the sign has been found, generally only one value need be calculated, unless a large error in magnitude suggests the last sign estimate was incorrect.

4.4.2 Error analysis

Equations 4.14 and 4.13 have the same right-hand side. 4.14 may be used whenever the absolute value of the right-hand side is less than or equal to 0.5, and 4.13 may be used whenever the absolute value of the right-hand side is greater than 0.5. In this case, the error of the calculation of theta is bound by the right-hand side of Equation 4.14,

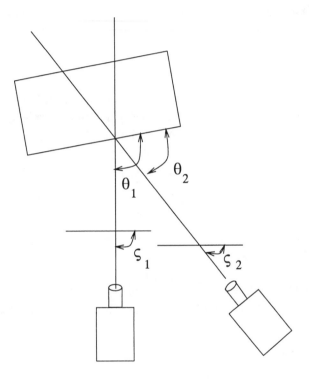

Figure 4.13: The change in θ and ς after the robot has moved.

and 4.13. ($\cos \theta$ and $\sin \theta$ are a less than linear mapping in this region.)
Thus, for both Equation 4.14 and 4.13,

$$Error(\theta) <= Error(\frac{\Delta Z_m \Delta u}{\Delta v \sqrt{X^2 + Y^2}}) \qquad (4.17)$$

Note that for the right-hand side of this equation to be less than or equal to 0.5, the angle of the object surface to the image plane must be 60°, thus, in practise Equation 4.14 is almost always used.

Now, ΔZ_m and X and Y all come from the model and are assumed to be accurate, thus

$$Error(\theta) <= Error(k\frac{\Delta u}{\Delta v}), \qquad (4.18)$$

where k is a constant. Let the error in Δu be ϵ_u, and the error in Δv be ϵ_v, then the relative error in Δu is $\frac{\epsilon_u}{\Delta u}$, let this be referred to as ϵ_{ru}, and similarly the relative error in Δv be ϵ_{rv}. Thus,

$$Error(\theta) <= \epsilon_{ru} + \epsilon_{rv}. \qquad (4.19)$$

For the error in Equation 4.15:

$$Error(\overline{T}_y) = Error(\frac{f \Delta Z_m}{\Delta v} + \overline{Y}_m \sin \theta + \overline{X}_m \cos \theta), \qquad (4.20)$$

Assume that the distance from the object is larger than the displacement of the points on the object, then $\frac{f \Delta Z_m}{\Delta v}$ is the major component of $\overline{T}_y$, thus:

$$Error(\overline{T}_y) \approx Error(\frac{f \Delta Z_m}{\Delta v}), \qquad (4.21)$$

Thus, removing constants:

$$Error(\overline{T}_y) \approx \epsilon_v \qquad (4.22)$$

The error in $\overline{T}_x$ may be large relative to $\overline{T}_x$, however, as the camera is centred on the object, $\overline{T}_x$ will typically not be large.

Thus, the estimates of θ and $\overline{T}_y$ are stable with respect to estimation errors in the image coordinates.

The error in the estimate of the sign of θ is equal to the error in the estimate of $\delta\varsigma$ (the change of angle of the pan platform with respect to odometric coordinates) if the camera axis intersects with exactly the same point on the object for both estimates. Clearly, this will seldom be the case. $\overline{T}_x$ could be used to calculate the error in the angle of the axis, but the error in $\overline{T}_x$ may be large. The error then must include an estimate of the largest possible error in $\delta\varsigma$ which would still allow a correct match. Figure 4.14 shows the intersection of the camera axis with the object for camera angles that would allow all the points on the object to appear in the image. For model matching, all matched points are clearly visible in the image. The differences between the angles of the two extreme views shows the possible range of $\delta\varsigma$ that would still lead to a correct match. Let η be the total angle subtended by the image, and let φ be the angle subtended by the object in the image, then the error in the estimate of θ_2 will be less than $\beta = \eta - \varphi$, plus the error in our estimate of $\delta\varsigma$:

$$Error(\theta_2) <= Error(\delta\varsigma) + (\eta - \varphi). \qquad (4.23)$$

For the experiments presented in Chapter 8, this bound β was generally less than 10 degrees. The sign can only be wrongly predicted within β of zero.

4.5   Conclusion

This chapter presented canonical-views, a novel viewer-centred object representation designed specifically for robot navigation. Canonical-views support causal view prediction through causal indexing. This allows the next view to be predicted based on the last view seen, and the robot motion since the view was seen. The chapter also derived a fast algebraic method for pose determination, and an analysis of the error of this determination. The methods presented facilitate the robot navigation system of this book. Chapter 5 presents the edge extraction, segmentation and matching techniques that support the object recognition method of the present chapter. Chapter 6 describes a technique for knowledge-based shape-from-shading, based on the canonical-views object model that is designed to be integrated with the system presented in this chapter.

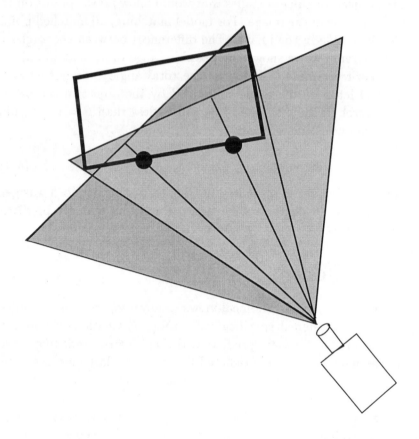

Figure 4.14: From a single camera location, this figure shows the two possible extremes of camera angle that would still allow all the object points to be visible.

Chapter 5

Edge Segmentation and Matching

This chapter describes the edge segmentation and matching technique that was developed to support the canonical-views modelling method described in Chapter 4. Specifically, Section 1 presents the edge segmentation algorithm and Section 2 presents the matching algorithm. The Canny edge detector was used for initial edge extraction. The methods here have been developed specifically to support extraction and matching for a ground-based mobile robot.

The edge extraction and matching techniques presented here have been designed specifically to support vision guided mobile robot navigation. The features are extracted before matching begins (see Figure 5.1). These techniques adequately handle spurious and broken edges, and are sufficiently fast to enable continuous robot movement when matching succeeds[1].

5.1 Edge Extraction

This section presents a method for extracting straight-line edges from an intensity image for subsequent model matching. The method has some similarities to the fast line finder [125], emphasising selective processing and ordering computation to reduce processing. Also, it uses

---

[1]1.6Hz on an Alphaserver 8400 for an indoor robot that moves at approximately 10cm per sec.

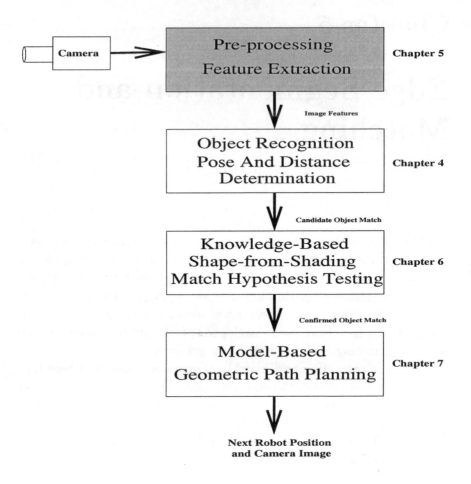

Figure 5.1: This chapter describes the edge segmentation and matching component of the architecture.

coarse quantisation into gradient buckets, and connected components analysis. However, it differs in that it is specific for mobile robot navigation, taking advantage of restricted rotation of edges given two dimensional robot motion, and using constraints from *apriori* object model knowledge. Further differences include processing edge segments rather than pixels, and quantising by ρ as well as gradient direction. Lebegue and Aggarwal [139] presented a method for straight-line extraction that takes a different approach, finding chains by pixel linking and recursively fitting lines by least squares.

The edge extraction and matching process is designed for reliability and real-time operation. Efficient processing is achieved by three general design features:

- Analyse edges at a scale that is coarse relative to image resolution, without excessive loss of resolution in edge location. (Operate on edge segments rather than edge pixels).

- Quantise edge segments by orientation and position into buckets that are likely to contain only segments from a single edge, which greatly reduces the amount of comparison between edge segments required for segment linking.

- Avoid computation that can be eliminated by use of model knowledge, and robot positional knowledge.

5.1.1   Edge extraction

Figure 5.2 shows the basic architecture. As a starting point, the Canny edge extractor [38] is applied to the raw image, followed by dual threshold edge synthesis, which gives a good quality initial edge image.

Finding straight-line segments

Firstly, the image is divided into a grid of windows each containing n x n pixels, as shown in Figure 5.3. A linear regression [183] is applied separately to each window. If there are less than $\frac{n}{k}$ edge pixels within the window the regression may not be meaningful, and the window is discarded. Errors in low-level edge extraction frequently leads to the loss of isolated pixels, results of the linear regression will not be excessively effected provided this number is small. For the experiments presented k was set to 2. The result of this process is a map of edge segments, one for each window with more than $\frac{n}{k}$ edge pixels.

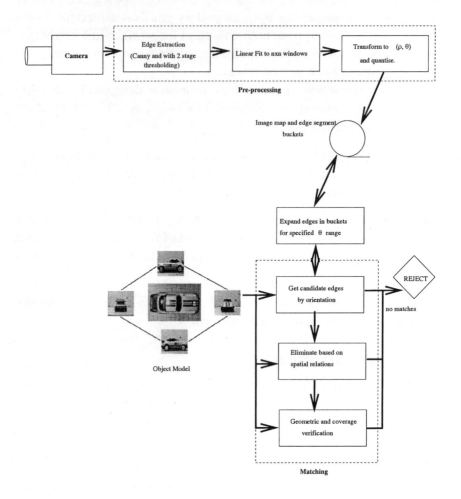

Figure 5.2: The edge extraction and matching architecture.

Quantisation of edge segments by ρ, θ

The linear regression parameters are unsuitable for direct quantisation as the y-intercept is local, and gradient is non-linear. Thus, gradient and y-intercept are transformed into ρ, θ coordinates, see Figure 5.4. Transformation from gradient to θ is performed using coarse lookup tables to increase speed. Figures 5.5 (a) and (b) show the coarse quantisation of θ and ρ into evenly spaced intervals. We adopt the term *bucket* for these intervals from [125]. Each window edge segment that has a fit error less than a threshold is allocated to a bucket based on ρ and θ values. Two separate indices of the edge segments are maintained, these are: an index to the segments contained in each ρ and θ bucket; and a spatial map indexing each segment by its image position. While the buckets contain only segments with satisfactory fit errors, the spatial map contains all edge segments regardless of error.

After this pre-processing stage, fusing of odometry information and previous position estimations, and use model-based matching reduce the amount of processing. Each match performed gives an estimate of the current view, as discussed in Chapter 4. The system only matches edges from the estimated view in the first instance. Due to the restricted rotation of the object relative to the robot, as described in Chapter 4, each edge can only appear within a finite range of possible angles which corresponds to a small fraction of the total number of buckets. The matching subsystem designates an angle range for candidate edges based on the edges to be matched in the view. The edge subsystem only expands edges in these ranges.

Expanding edges within buckets

Consider that for a particular bucket, there is a set, E, of all edge segments, e_i, that have $\theta^l \leq \theta < \theta^u$, and $\rho^l \leq \rho < \rho^u$. Note that the subscript here indicates an index. Superscripts will be used as labels. End-points cannot be found by just taking the two $e_i \in E$ that are most distant apart in the image because within E there may be segments from several distinct edges, as shown in Figure 5.6 (a).[2]

Parallel edges may occur within a single window, in which case the edges are merged by the windowing process (see Figure 5.6 (b)). The same edge pair may fall into separate windows depending on their

---

[2]Spurious edge segments are infrequent due to rejection based on fit error, and the minimum edge pixel requirement.

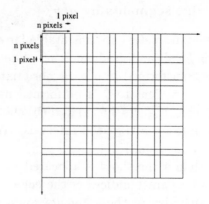

Figure 5.3: A portion of the image which is divided into overlapping n x n windows. The windows overlap by one pixel to prevent edges that run along the border between two windows being fragmented.

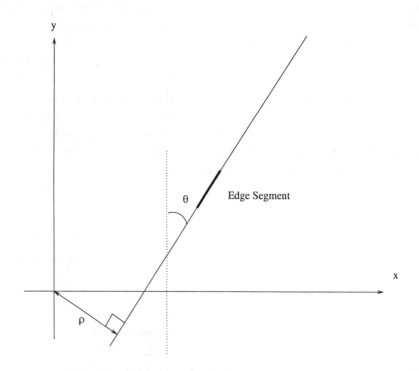

Figure 5.4: The quantisation parameters. ρ is the minimum distance from the origin, and θ is the absolute angle.

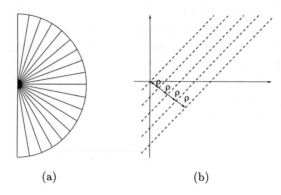

Figure 5.5: (a) Orientation is quantised into ten degree buckets. (b) ρ is quantised into thirty pixel buckets. This shows quantisation of ρ for a constant value of theta.

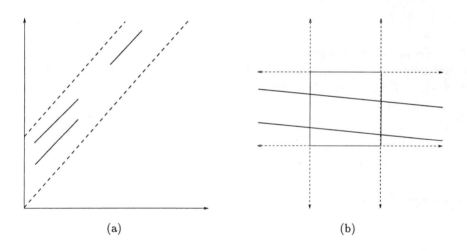

Figure 5.6: (a) Multiple edge segments may fall within a single bucket, either: spatially separated along the principal direction (θ) of the bucket; or narrowly separated edges running parallel to each other. (b) Parallel edges that appear within a single window will not be discriminated.

position with respect to window boundaries. In this case, it would be consistent to merge these two lines. However, in implementation $\rho^u - \rho^l$ is up to six times the size of the window width. Thus, parallel edge pairs with perpendicular separation considerably greater than one window may fall within a single bucket. In this case they should not be merged.

If there are parallel edges within a bucket, then the component segments of each parallel line form distinct subsets. Formally, we may define a partition of the edge segments in a bucket based on collinearity, as shown in Figure 5.7.

Definition 3 *Let $C(a, b)$ be the symmetric relation[3] that b appears on the line defined by the edge segment a. Given the set, E, of edge segments allocated to a bucket, the partition is defined by a collection of subsets E^p of E where:*

$$E^p = \{a \in E, b \in E \mid C(a, b)\}.$$

Thus, for each bucket E, we have a set of zero or more subsets E^p. Each E^p contains the segments of a parallel line that falls within the bucket.

In practice, if edge segment b appears on the line defined by edge segment a, it is not necessarily the case that a appears on the line defined by b due to the discrete nature of the image and possible spurious or missing edge pixels. Thus, because C is not reflexive, the subsets, E^p, are not necessarily mutually disjoint, and thus do not form a partition in the formal algebraic sense. However, this definition is adequate in most cases to separate the parallel lines within a bucket.

Edge segment linking

Given a subset of collinear edge segments within a bucket, spatial connectivity must be examined in order to find the complete edges. Segments of a partition subset are linked by finding a path of intermediate edge segments between them. The notion of a path is formalised in the next section.

To this end, the edge segments of a partition subset are first sorted in image space along the principal direction of the bucket. Attempting

---

[3]Symmetric in the formal algebraic sense, i.e., if $C(a, b)$ then $C(b, a)$ for $a, b \in X$, where C is a relation and X is a set [101].

to join the segments that are closest to each other first prevents computation being wasted in finding a path that has been found earlier in a failed attempt to link distant edge segments. Sorting the edge segments forms an ordered set $e_1...e_n$, where n is the number of segments in a partition subset. Paths are then sought between each segment e_k, and the other edge segments e_l, where $l > k$, starting with e_{k+1}.[4] Frequently a path cannot be found from e_k to e_{k+1}, but a path can be found to e_{k+2} due to the discrete nature of the edge segments, as depicted in Figure 5.8.

Quantisation in edge parameter space is important due to the computational complexity of edge linking. Linking may require $O(n^2)$ searches for straight-line connecting paths in the worst case, where n is the number of edge segments in the bucket.[5] In the experiments presented in this book, quantisation restricted n to be generally less than ten, and almost never greater than 20.

While searching for straight-line connected components, it is not sufficient to examine the segments of a single bucket for two key reasons: 1) edgels from a single edge may appear in several buckets (see Figure 5.9); and 2) edge segments may be allocated to the wrong bucket. The second problem is caused by regression errors due to spurious or missing pixels because edge extraction is imperfect for real images. Even without errors, edge junctions cause problems for simple linear regression. These difficulties are accepted as a trade off for simplifying initial processing.

Finding paths to connect edge segments

Typically, connected components analysis [125, 191] is used to analyse pixel connectivity. However, the method presented here deals with edge segments, so the analysis must be modified accordingly.

First some definitions from [191] are presented, modified to apply to edge segments rather than edgels:

Definition 4 *In an image consisting of uniform rectangular elements, a unit element of an image at location (x, y) has a set of points called the* **8-neighbours** *associated with it. These are at locations: $(x - 1, y), (x, y - 1), (x, y + 1), (x + 1, y), (x - 1, y - 1), (x - 1, y + 1), (x + 1, y - 1), (x + 1, y + 1)$.*

---

[4]Pairs will already have been tested for $l \leq k$.

[5]For example, this will occur if no edge segments actually link.

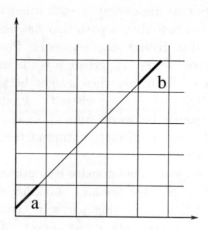

Figure 5.7: a and b are collinear, or $c(a, b)$, if a appears on the line defined by b, and b appears on the line defined by a.

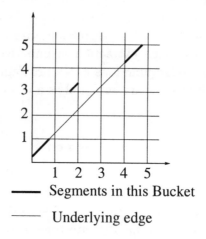

——— Segments in this Bucket

——— Underlying edge

Figure 5.8: Let the edge segment at (0,0) be e_k, the segment at (2,3) be e_{k+1}, and the segment at (4,4) be e_{k+2}. Both e_k and e_{k+2} are on the same line, and the linking process will find a path between them if the edge has been extracted correctly in the intermediate windows. This figure shows that e_{k+1} is not part of this edge, and will not be linked successfully to e_k. Clearly, it is important to continue attempting to find paths to segments e_{k+n}, where $n > 1$.

Definition 5 *A path π of length n from P to Q in $\sum$ is a sequence of points $P = P_0, P_1, ..., P_n = Q$, such that P_i is an 8-neighbour of P_{i-1}, $1 \leq i \leq n$.*

Definition 6 *Let S be a subset of $\sum$, and let P and Q be points of S. We say that P is connected to Q in S if there exists a path from P to Q consisting entirely of points of S. For any P in S, the set of points that are connected to P in S is called a connected component of S (see Figure 5.10 (a)).*

However, in this chapter, only straight edges are extracted, and the unit elements are edge segments. Thus a variation on the above definition is required.

Definition 7 *Let S be the subset of $\sum$, and let P and Q be points of S. We say that P is straight-line connected to Q if P and Q are connected and all the points on the path from P to Q are intersected by the infinitely long line $\overline{PQ}$. For any P in S, the set of points connected to P in S is called a straight-line connected component of S (see Figure 5.10 (b)).*

Thus, in order for there to be a straight-line edge segment between e_k and e_l, e_k and e_l must be straight-line connected, and the edge segments that form the straight-line connection must be consistent in ρ and θ with e_k and e_l.

Implementation

Let $e_b \in \{e_k, e_l\}$ with parameters (ρ_b, θ_b) be the base segment for the linking process, such that the other edge segment is on the line defined by (ρ_b, θ_b), the parameters of e_b. To determine which edge segments are intersected by the line joining e_k and e_l, (ρ_b, θ_b) are used. For a candidate edge segment to be straight-line connected, it must satisfy the following criteria:

- there are more than $\frac{n}{k}$ edge pixels in the window (condition for a fit to occur);

and either of:

1. $\theta(e_b) + \theta_t <= \theta(e_c) - \theta_{err}(e_c)$ or $\theta(e_b) - \theta_t <= \theta(e_c) + \theta_{err}(e_c)$ (see Figure 5.11); or,

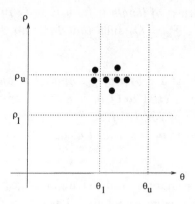

Figure 5.9: Most edge segments for an edge appear in a single bucket in (ρ, θ) space. However, because the boundaries are crisp, an edge that is near the boundaries of a bucket may have some segments that appear in other nearby buckets. A straight line near boundaries in ρ and θ may appear in four buckets, as shown, due to the digitisation of the edges. Straight lines are unlikely to appear spread over more than four buckets unless the bucket size is a similar scale to the digitisation of the image, (ignoring fit errors).

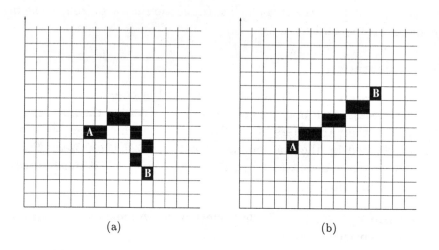

Figure 5.10: (a) A and B are connected by a path of edge pixels; and (b) A and B are straight-line connected.

2. it satisfies a pixel-based linear fit, i.e., more than np pixels within the window fall on the line defined by (ρ_b, θ_b).[6]

Condition 2, shown above, allows a pixel-based fit, particularly to account for edge intersections that fall within a window.

The requirement that there must be a path between e_i and e_j is relaxed in order to allow gaps of a single window. This enables the method to tolerate bad linear regression results for single windows. However, some pairs of collinear edges that are actually separated will be joined. The matching scheme is tolerant of this problem, allowing the same image edge to match multiple model edges.

Note, it is not problematic that the segments of an edge may be distributed over several buckets by quantisation, as long as two component segments fall into a single bucket edge linking will still occur. A pathological case where an edge consists of four edgels, each of which resides in a separate bucket, would result in the edge being lost.

Edge End-Point Extension

Once an edge has been found, this method attempts to extend each end-point of the edge by linking more edge segments at either end. Edge segments that are straight-line connected to the extrapolation of $\overline{PQ}$ are linked, see Figure 5.12. The true pixel coordinates of the end-points are found within the end edge segments of the final expanded edge. The loss of a few pixels due to a missing partial window the end of an extracted edge is not important because the matching method does not require exact end-points of the edge.

5.1.2 On the choice of window size and quantisation of ρ and θ

Figure 5.13 shows that choice of window size affects the smallest strip edge that can be reliably distinguished from a single line. There is no general maximal width of strip that should be merged into a single edge. For robot navigation, we must consider the size of the features we are interested in, and embodied parameters of the robot[7] in selecting the maximal window size. As a model-based method is used, the model

---

[6]p was set to $\frac{2}{3}$ in the experiments presented in this book

[7]These were discussed Chapter 3 and include the scale at which the robot will view these features given the pixel resolution, zoom capabilities, and required robot-to-object distances.

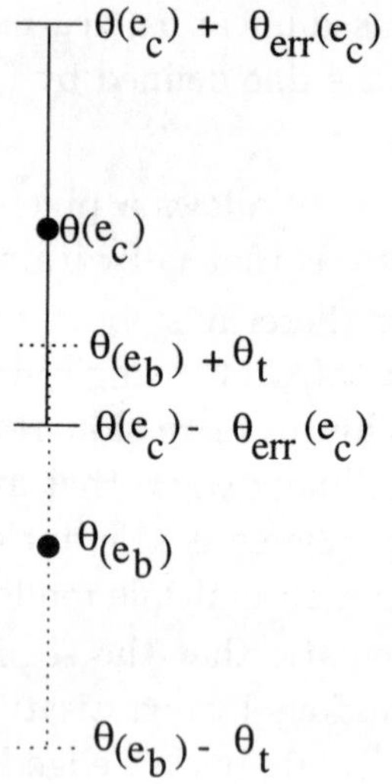

$$\theta(e_c) + \theta_{err}(e_c)$$

$$\theta(e_c)$$

$$\theta(e_b) + \theta_t$$

$$\theta(e_c) - \theta_{err}(e_c)$$

$$\theta(e_b)$$

$$\theta(e_b) - \theta_t$$

Figure 5.11: $\theta(e_b)$ is the parameter from e_b, the base edge segment for this linking process, and θ_t is the constant error threshold. $\theta(e_c)$ is the parameter of the candidate, and $\theta_{err}(e_c)$ is the error associated with the linear fit for the candidate (converted from gradient space). The match is accepted if the error bounds for θ for the candidate, $\theta(e_c)$, fall within an acceptable threshold of $\theta(e_b)$.

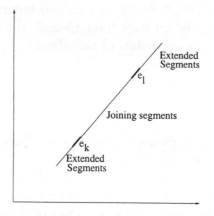

Figure 5.12: The expanding process has linked the starting segments e_k, e_l to find the basic edge, then additional segments have been found at either end that are straight-line connected to the e_k and e_l to extend the edge.

must account for the parameters of the robot, the camera, and clearly the image processing choices that are made.[8]

The width of the intervals of quantisation of ρ and θ directly affects the distribution of edge segments into buckets. Narrow quanta lead to fewer segments falling into each bucket, which may lead to the segments of a single edge being distributed across many buckets. Alternatively, large quanta may lead to segments from many edges falling into a single bucket, which may increase the computational complexity of path finding. Quantisation intervals of 30 pixels for ρ, and ten degrees for θ were found to be effective for the experimental scenarios documented in this book.

5.2 Edge Matching

This section describes how the edges that were extracted in section 6.1 are matched to a model. It is well known that edge extraction is an unreliable process, and that frequently only partial edges can be recovered. Further, edges may be partially occluded, or partly hidden by specular reflection under normal indoor lighting. The edge matching method presented here aims to match edges reliably, when only part of the edges may have been extracted, assuming that some part of every edge is extracted. The intersections of the component extracted edges are taken, and assess the geometry of candidate matches based on the intersections, rather than the extracted edges (see Figure 5.15). This requires that edges on which the geometric assessment of the match is to be made must intersect with other edges.

5.2.1 Evaluating matches

A cluttered image can lead to an enormous number of edges generating many thousands of possible match candidates (see Figure 5.14). These candidates can be evaluated by several criteria:

1. Basic spatial properties of the edges, and their spatial relations to the other edges;

---

[8]If close parallel strips needed to be separated, the presence of multiple edges could be detected by the distribution of pixels in the n x n window. In this case, the window could be split into four (n/2) x (n/2) windows recursively down to the scale of a single pixel. However, the system does not pursue this course as it is an expensive overhead.

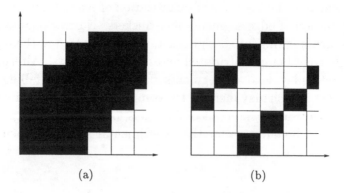

(a)   (b)

Figure 5.13: A narrow strip appearing in the image (a) may result in two edges that fall within a single window as shown in (b).

(a)   (b)

Figure 5.14: (a) An image of a car with little background clutter; and (b) the 217 segmented straight edges that are extracted from it. The model of the side surface of the car contains eight edges, leading to potentially 217^8 possible candidates.

2. To what degree the extracted candidate edges cover the model edges;

3. How well does the geometry of the hypothesised match fit in with a geometric model of the object; and

4. How well does the estimate of object position, that arises from the match, coincide with what we know the position to be based estimates from previous matches, given recent odometric readings.

Suppose that there are m edges in the model to be matched, and c candidate edges are extracted from the image, then there will be c^m candidate matches, see Figure 5.14. To match in a reasonable time the combinatorial explosion must be controlled. Operations that require the least computation in order to eliminate the largest number of matches must be performed first.

5.2.2   Spatial elimination

Grimson [89] discusses the relative restrictions on orientation of edges for matching given six degrees of freedom of relative motion between camera and object. However, given the restricted motion of the robot with respect to the object, absolute restrictions on orientation of the edges may be employed. Each object edge can only appear within a finite range of possible orientations in the image. The edge extraction method presented in Section 6.1 only extracts edges within the required ranges of orientation. Thus, the vast majority of match candidates need never be considered at all.

Evaluating basic spatial relations between the edges only requires integer point comparisons, and is used next to eliminate candidates. Nine binary operands are employed: LEFTOF, RIGHTOF, ABOVE, BELOW, LEFTOF1, RIGHTOF1, ABOVE1, BELOW1, COLINEAR. These are described in Chapter 4. Candidate matches that fail any spatial constraint are eliminated.

5.2.3   Edge coverage

Figure 5.15 shows a set of extracted edges that are being matched to a trapezoid. For a partial edge to be evaluated, it is generally required that the edge intersect with one other edge at both endpoints in the

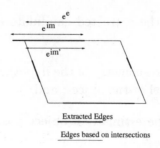

Figure 5.15: Based on the candidate edges and the model, intersections are calculated to find the match for geometric evaluation. There are three lengths for each of the edges: e^i, the edge extracted from the image; e^e, the edge that terminates at its intersections with connecting edges from the model; and $e^{i'}$, the part of e^i that overlaps e^e. The coverage ratio is $\frac{e_i{}'}{e_e}$.

model.[9] Calculating the intersections' coordinates for the image edges gives the prediction of the underlying object edges for this candidate match. Edges extracted from the image will not always cover the entire length of what can be seen as the true edge. Thus, there are three sets of edges, e^e, e^{im}, and $e^{im'}$ as shown in Figure 5.15. Given ideal edge extraction e^{im} and e^e would be identical, but, in practice, typically e^{im} will be shorter. $e^{i'}$ is formed, to cover the occasions when the extracted edge is longer than the intersecting edge. For each $e^{im'}$ the coverage ratio is:

$$e^c = \frac{||e^{im'}||}{||e^e||} \qquad (5.1)$$

A composite of e^c for all edges matched is used to evaluate match candidate, allowing one poorly extracted edge by ignoring the edge for which e^c is a minimum. Thus, given a set of n edges in a candidate match, the measure of coverage for the match, c^m, is defined:

$$c^m = \frac{\sum_{i=0}^{n} e_i^c - min(e_i^c)}{n - 1}, \qquad (5.2)$$

where $0 < c^m \leq 1$, and the minimum e_i^c is the minimum value of

---

[9]The model does allow non-connecting edges but these cannot be geometrically evaluated, and so will only contribute to discrimination based on their orientation and relative position.

the set $e_0^c, e_1^c, ...e_n^c$. Matches where c^m is less than a constant threshold, c^t, are rejected without further evaluation. c^t was set to 0.5 in the experiments presented.

5.2.4 Position estimation consistency

Each candidate match that satisfies the basic spatial constraints gives an estimate of object position. The object is stationary and so remains fixed in the robot's odometric coordinate system, other than odometric drift. The time between robot assessments of object position is small, and so although odometric error grows without bound over time, the error accumulated between processing images is bounded. The difference between two estimates of object position transformed into odometric coordinates is equal to the odometric error plus the errors in the estimations of object position. Thus, we may fuse data from vision and odometry to evaluate candidate matches.

5.2.5 Geometric verification

Geometric verification of matches for the general case is discussed by Grimson [89]. This is a special case due to the restricted rotation relation discussed in Chapter 4. In this book, geometric verification is performed by calculating the pose associated with a candidate match, and checking that the pose is consistent with the robot motion, and that all points in the candidate match are consistent with the pose. Checking is implemented by projecting the model edges into a virtual image, based on the pose estimate. The similarity between the virtual image and the real image is then measured by the total least squared differences in the length of the normalised edges, and on the sum of the absolute difference of the angles.

First the pose is evaluated. Let ζ be the difference between the estimate of relative orientation of the object based on the match and that predicted by the last match and odometry. If ζ is greater than a threshold amount, ζ^{max} the match is rejected. If orientation differs by less than the maximum threshold, but more than a lower threshold ζ^{min} the match is penalised by g^{m1}:

$$g^{m1} = c * (\zeta - \zeta^{min}), \tag{5.3}$$

where c is a constant. c was set to 2 and ζ was measured in radians in the experiments presented.

A similar process takes place for the estimate of the relative position of the object to find a penalty g^{m2}.

Let (x, y, z) be the coordinates of a model point that has correspondences with image points in a match, then the virtual image point p_i^m is:

$$p^m = (\frac{f(y \cos \theta - x \sin \theta)}{depth - x \cos \theta - y \sin \theta}, \frac{fz}{depth - x \cos \theta - y \sin \theta}), \quad (5.4)$$

where θ is the orientation of the model with respect to the object.

Let e_i^v be the edges that arise from connecting the points p_i^m according to the model. The measure of length verification g^{m1} is:

$$g^{m3} = \sum_{i=0}^{n} || \frac{e_i^v}{\sum_{i=0}^{n} ||e_i^v||} - \frac{e_i^e}{\sum_{i=0}^{n} ||e_i^v||} ||, \quad (5.5)$$

and angle verification g^{m2} is performed as follows:

$$g^{m4} = \sum_{i=0}^{n} \cos^{-1} \frac{e_i^v.e_i^e}{||e_i^v||.||e_i^e||} \quad (5.6)$$

All the geometric verification measures are combined:

$$g^m = \frac{g^{m1} + g^{m2} + g^{m3} + g^{m4}}{g^n}, \quad (5.7)$$

where g^n is a constant to normalise g^m. Matches with g^m greater than a threshold will be rejected.

To combine g^c and g^m, we subtract the threshold, c^t, from c^m, and normalise the result to increase the discrimination between candidates based on coverage, without increasing its emphasis overall. This is added to the normalised result of the combination of the geometric measures, to form the evaluation of the match e^m:

$$e^m = \frac{c^m - c^t}{1 - c^t} + g^m. \quad (5.8)$$

We find e^m for all matches m^i, and take the minimum:

$$m^s = MIN_{i=0}^{p} e^m. \quad (5.9)$$

5.2.6 Quadratic edge extraction

If required, the system is able to extract curved edges. The system segments edges extracted by the Canny Edge detector into lines of near uniform curvature. Short initial line segments are extrapolated by fitting quadratic curves using Neville's algorithm [183]. Extrapolation terminates when the interpolation error exceeds a certain threshold, corresponding to a corner (sharp change in curvature). This method is substantially slower than that presented above, and is only used if required. Cubic interpolation is not used as it is rather unreliable.

5.2.7 Further active processing

Given that a stream of images from a camera is being processed, it may be possible to restrict processing further by only extracting edges in likely locations for edges given previous images. Windowing-based tracking methods could be applied, but this has not been explored in this book.

Chapter 6

Knowledge Based Shape from Shading

Edge-based matching can differentiate many objects, however, it is inadequate for discriminating objects with a similar wire-frame. This chapter presents a method for extracting the shape of an object from a single image when knowledge about the object is available. The main application in our architecture is for shape-based verification of edge-based matches, where shape derived from the image will be checked against the shape for the candidate model view of the object. A second application is where a robot needs to recover object shape when it has only a wire-frame model,[1] and it has to move close to the object due to obstacles or task requirements. Navigating entirely on the basis of the wire-frame may lead to a collision with a convex curved surface, even though the robot is clear of the object as modelled by the wire-frame, as shown in Figure 6.1.

Although the shape-from-shading problem has been studied extensively, this chapter argues that each class of existing solutions is inadequate to support the robot navigation of the system presented in this book. This chapter describes a novel method for extracting the shape of an object. This method fits the two requirements of the system: 1) testing view-match candidate hypotheses; and 2) extracting shape under partial modelling. This chapter also illustrates the benefits of using a knowledge-based approach to low-level image processing tasks.

---

[1] A wire-frame model models only the boundaries of object surfaces and not the shape of the surfaces themselves

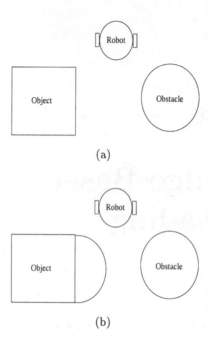

Figure 6.1: (a) Based on the wire-frame model of the object, the robot may expect to be able to pass between the object and the obstacle, however, in (b), once the shape of the object is known, it is clear that the robot cannot pass through the gap.

6.1 Introduction

The importance of applying domain knowledge to artificial intelligence (AI) programs has been a fundamental observation arising from research in AI [78]. This observation has been applied to many areas of computer vision, as discussed in Chapter 2. However, in general, the use of knowledge for early vision processing has been restricted. Few systems use constraints from a knowledge-base directly in image operators, as opposed to controlling the application of the operators. Early vision processing has focussed primarily on precognitive methods where a generic operator is applied to the image based on some assumptions about the image formation process and generic properties of what appears.

As discussed in Chapter 2, most shape-from-shading research takes the classical computer vision approach: analysing a single static image without the use of knowledge. This chapter demonstrates the efficacy of the knowledge-based approach to tasks of early vision, particularly shape-from-shading. This chapter shows that the knowledge-based approach can give advantages both in terms of what problems can be solved, and of computational time. Three different forms of knowledge are applied: object model; processing rules; and, knowledge-based domain-specific initialisation. Object model knowledge provides an additional constraint, or boundary condition. This enables the method to find solutions for objects where no singular points or occluding boundaries are visible, but orientation discontinuities are visible, for which the angle between the two surface normals at the boundary is known.

Rule-based processing is used to automate the process of shape-from-shading. Knowledge-based domain-specific initialisation allows the algorithm to converge more quickly than comparable algorithms, and ensures that it converges to the correct solution when several solutions are possible. The use of knowledge in the operation of an early vision operator represents a new paradigm in computer vision. The results for simulated images with noise and real camera images are presented in order to demonstrate the effectiveness of the approach.

In order to apply knowledge to shape-from-shading, a knowledge-based architecture based on frame constructs [160] is employed. Note, however, that this is not a traditional application of frames, shape-from-shading operates on numeric rather than symbolic data, and knowledge, in this case, consists of both symbolic and numeric data.

6.1.1 Motivation and system perspective

In the system presented in this book, shape determination is used to compare the shape against a model to verify a match hypothesised by edge matching before navigation proceeds (see Figure 6.2). A second possible function, in the context of vision-guided mobile robot navigation, is to estimate the protrusion of the object beyond its wire frame, based on the shape. This can be applied during navigation and manipulation tasks when the robot is operating close to an object and only a partial object model (e.g., edges) is available. This idea is not explored further in this book.

Under view-based recognition, the observer can recognise a particular view only from a restricted region of view space. If this region is small, it may be possible to verify that the shading is consistent

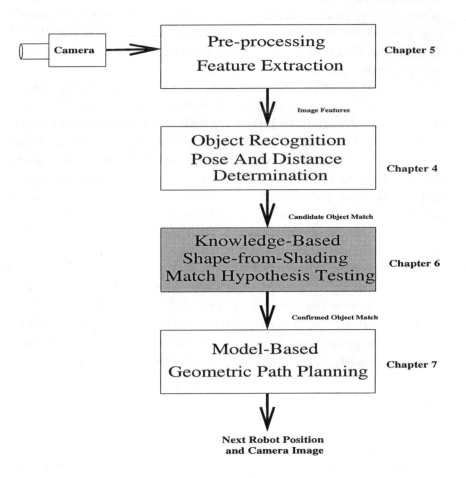

Figure 6.2: This chapter describes the Knowledge-Based Shape-from-Shading shape verification.

with the expected shape. However, this region can be quite large for canonical-views and the estimation of object pose is only approximate as discussed in Chapter 4. The angle between the camera axis and the surface normal at any point may vary by a significant amount across a large region of view-space. Verification becomes complex without a strong restriction on the possible angle of the surface normal, especially for highly curved surfaces. This chapter considers this problem, and explores advantages that can be yielded by taking a knowledge-based approach to the shape-from-shading problem, particularly, when combined with edge-based matching. In the present system, shape-from-shading is applied after edge-based matching. The object is pre-segmented into smooth surfaces along orientation discontinuities.

In general, most existing shape-from-shading research focuses on reconstruction of three-dimensional shape, which is a time consuming process. This type of process is a typical example of general vision, as discussed in Chapter 3, where a system attempts to extract information suitable for *any* purpose. This chapter examines the extraction of shape for object recognition for the navigation of an autonomous mobile robot. The requirements of the robot system must be taken into consideration as shape-from-shading is an integral part of the robotic system. These include:

- The system is required to work quickly, ideally in real-time, so the robot should not pause for too long processing a single view of the object;

- The system needs to find an approximation to the shape of the object, not the precise shape;

- The system must require no manual intervention as the robot is autonomous; and

- The shape description is required for model-matching, and the calculation of the approximate extent of surface beyond the basic object wire-frame. Therefore, unlike traditional shape-from-shading, full reconstruction is unnecessary.

Autonomous robots require a fast shape-from-shading method that can operate without human intervention, finding information specifically for the purposes of object matching, and estimation of protrusion. Surface normals are adequate as the primary product of shape-from-shading. The system must also satisfy some other constraints particular to the problem presented, which make other methods in the literature inappropriate.

For mobile robot object recognition, existing variational methods are inadequate as many manufactured objects have planar, or near planar faces, that have no occluding limb boundaries, and are unlikely, in general, to have points of singular brightness. Similarly, the method of Oliensis [171] requires one or more points of singular brightness, and so cannot be applied directly to such cases. Malik and Maydan [152] rely on the availability of a sparse labelled edge diagram, but edge labelling is not reliable from edges extracted from a raw image. The linear surface reflectance assumption is problematic for robot vision. The camera axis and the light-source direction may be close if the light-source is mounted on the robot. Further, noise is often a problem with real cameras. Local methods require assumptions about local surface geometry. It is too restrictive to assume that all objects of interest have a particular local surface shape. Finally, many of the three-dimensional reconstruction methods discussed above generally implicitly rely on user intervention. Variational methods require boundary conditions to be set manually, while local methods require the selection of an appropriate model for local shape.

6.1.2   Assumptions

As the shape-from-shading algorithm presented in this chapter is used as an integrated part of a robot system, rather than stand-alone, some things can be reasonably assumed to be in the system's model. These assumptions are stated explicitly in this section to clarify the generality of the algorithm presented.

The model provides the correspondences between the pixel location of edges and a geometric model. The edges are extracted and matched in this case by the method presented in Chapter 4. The model provides the angles between surfaces along the discontinuities, the light source direction, and the albedo for each surface. Methods for estimation presented by other research [140, 141, 243], can be considered if light-source direction or albedo is unknown. This chapter describes a general formulation, but particularly examines the case where surfaces are approximately lambertian, with approximately constant albedo. Previous research reports the use of different lighting and reflection models [107, 163, 198] in cases where the lambertian model is not a good approximation.

6.1.3   Knowledge-based representation of objects

The approach to the shape-from-shading problem presented in this chapter requires the representation of knowledge about the visual appearance of the object as well as knowledge about properties of the object itself. Some correspondences between the geometric structures of the object and perceived structures in the image are also required. Further required facts are light source direction and knowledge derived from the image. This knowledge must be combined with control rules that govern the processing in the system, and the numerical processes that collectively form a shape solution for the object in the image. In specific domains knowledge about types of objects being examined may assist the solution process. Frames [160] are used as they allow packaging of declarative knowledge with procedural knowledge. Also, they allow the ability to group facts, rules and processes into associative clusters [88].

Requicha [187] presents methods for symbolic representation of three-dimensional solids. Boundary representations are used in this book, because most perceptual data for recognising objects occurs at boundaries and on surfaces. In boundary representations, objects are represented as collections of "faces" or "patches", which are described by bounding edges and vertices. Non-planar surfaces also require representation of the surface shape. In typical boundary schemes, the concept of a face may not correspond to what appears perceptually to be a face. Representations that model the object as perceived by the robot are more suitable for the system presented in this chapter.

6.2   Using Object Model Knowledge for Shape-From-Shading

In model-based computer vision, it is reasonable to assume that the object can be modelled as piecewise smooth, i.e., there are no discontinuities within faces, although there may be discontinuities between faces. Many manufactured objects are composed of smooth faces separated by discontinuities, and this is an adequate approximation for many natural objects.

The object model knowledge applied consists of the following aspects:

- A wire frame model of the object;

- The direction of faces of the object (what is inside and outside the object);

- The angle between adjoining object faces;

- A hypothesis as to which faces are visible in the image; and

- The correspondence between the edges in the model and those in the actual image.

6.3   A New Boundary Condition for Shape-From-Shading

The mathematical approach is based on that of Brooks and Horn [24], and expands the ideas of Malik and Maydan [152] of using a segmented image. The method proposed in this chapter is able to find a unique solution whenever part of an orientation discontinuity between two adjoining surfaces and the surfaces near the edge are visible. It also handles the limb and the singular point case. In addition, this method is also able to find a unique solution for the cases described in [24, 152] without user intervention.

If the angle between two surfaces along an edge is ϕ, then at a pair of pixels along an edge common to the two surfaces, the surface normals will be at an angle of $\theta = \phi - \pi$. Let the surface normal on the first surface be denoted as n_1 and the surface normal on the second surface as n_2. Now from vector geometry [101] we have:

$$n_1 \cdot n_2 = \| n_1 \| \cdot \| n_2 \| \cdot \cos \theta. \tag{6.1}$$

This can be simplified by restricting n_1 and n_2 to be unit vectors.

$$n_1 \cdot n_2 = \cos \theta. \tag{6.2}$$

Equation 6.2 provides an additional constraint on the orientation of the surface normals for the pixels along an edge.

Combining this equation with those used by Malik and Maydan: the image irradiance equations for each pixel; and the triple product of the normals and the direction of the edge gives four equations. A solution can now be found for the four unknowns. Most ambiguous solutions can be pruned through knowledge of whether each edge is concave or convex, and the fact that the surface normals for all visible points must be in the direction of the camera. Combining pruning with knowledge-based initialisation of surface normals generally leads to correct solutions. Direct iterative solutions such as Newton's method are too sensitive to noise, so variation is used. This method is similar to that in [24].

The image irradiance equations for the two surfaces are:

$$E_1 - R_1(\mathbf{n}_1) = 0, \tag{6.3}$$
$$E_2 - R_2(\mathbf{n}_2) = 0, \tag{6.4}$$

where E_1 and E_2 are the image intensities of pixels, and R_1 and R_2 are the reflectance maps of the first and second surfaces respectively.

Edges can be assumed to be smooth, as any discontinuities should be modelled. Smoothing is not required to produce a unique solution so it is not included for the purposes of this derivation. However, it has been applied in experiments with real images to suppress noise. Note, that the resulting surface normals could also be smoothed.

$$I(x, y) = \int \int_\Omega [(E_1 - R_1(\mathbf{n}_1))^2 + (E_2 - R_2(\mathbf{n}_2))^2 \tag{6.5}$$
$$+ \lambda_1(\mathbf{n}_1 \cdot \mathbf{n}_2 - \cos\theta)^2 + \lambda_2(\mathbf{n}_1\mathbf{n}_2\mathbf{Nc})^2$$
$$+ \mu_1(x, y)(\|\mathbf{n}_1\|) + \mu_2(x, y)(\|\mathbf{n}_2\|)]dxdy,$$

where $\mu_1(x, y)$ and $\mu_2(x, y)$ are Lagrange multipliers, and λ_1 and λ_2 are scalars giving the weight of the constraint terms.

To solve Equation (6.6) form two components, and update $\mathbf{n}_1$ and $\mathbf{n}_1$ in turn.

$$f(E_1, \mathbf{n}_1, \mathbf{n}_2, \theta, \mathbf{Nc}, \lambda_1, \lambda_2) = \int \int_\Omega [(E_1 - R_1(\mathbf{n}_1))^2 + (E_2 - R_2(\mathbf{n}_2))^2$$
$$+ \lambda_1(\mathbf{n}_1 \cdot \mathbf{n}_2 - \cos\theta)^2 + \lambda_2(\mathbf{n}_1\mathbf{n}_2\mathbf{Nc})^2$$
$$- \mu_1(x, y)(\|\mathbf{n}_1\|)]dxdy, \tag{6.6}$$

$$f(E_1, \mathbf{n}_1, \mathbf{n}_2, \theta, \mathbf{Nc}, \lambda_1, \lambda_2) = \int \int_\Omega [(E_1 - R_1(\mathbf{n}_1))^2 + (E_2 - R_2(\mathbf{n}_2))^2$$
$$+ \lambda_1(\mathbf{n}_1 \cdot \mathbf{n}_2 - \cos\theta)^2 + \lambda_2(\mathbf{n}_1\mathbf{n}_2\mathbf{Nc})^2$$
$$- \mu_2(x, y)(\|\mathbf{n}_2\|)]dxdy. \tag{6.7}$$

(6.6) and (6.7) can be solved by taking the Euler equations. The functional

$$\int\int_{\Omega} F(x, y, \mathbf{n})dxdy \qquad (6.8)$$

has the Euler equation

$$\mathbf{F_n} = 0. \qquad (6.9)$$

Thus, assuming that the reflectance map is differentiable, we may write the Euler equations for (6.6) and (6.7) as follows:

$$2(E_1 - R_1(\mathbf{n}_1))R_1'(\mathbf{n}_1) + 2(E_2 - R_2(\mathbf{n}_2))R_2'(\mathbf{n}_2)$$
$$+\lambda_1(\mathbf{n}_2(\mathbf{n}_1 \cdot \mathbf{n}_2 - \cos(\theta)) + \lambda_2(\mathbf{n}_1\mathbf{n}_2\mathbf{Nc})\mathbf{n}_{2_{i,j}} \times \mathbf{Nc} - \mu_1\mathbf{n}_1 = 0, (6.10)$$
$$2(E_1 - R_1(\mathbf{n}_1))R_1'(\mathbf{n}_1) + 2(E_2 - R_2(\mathbf{n}_2))R_2'(\mathbf{n}_2)$$
$$+\lambda_1(\mathbf{n}_1(\mathbf{n}_1 \cdot \mathbf{n}_2 - \cos(\theta)) + \lambda_2(\mathbf{n}_1\mathbf{n}_2\mathbf{Nc})\mathbf{n}_{1_{i,j}} \times \mathbf{Nc} - \mu_2\mathbf{n}_2 = 0, (6.11)$$

where $R_1'(\mathbf{n}_1), R_2'(\mathbf{n}_1)$ are derivatives with respect to $\mathbf{n}_1$, and $R_1'(\mathbf{n}_2)$, $R_2'(\mathbf{n}_2)$ are derivatives with respect to $\mathbf{n}_2$.

The factor of two may be incorporated into λ_1, λ_2 and the Lagrange multipliers. Now, evaluate (6.10) at pixels using the discrete form:

$$(E_{1_{i,j}} - R_1(\mathbf{n}_{1_{i,j}}))R_1'(\mathbf{n}_{1_{i,j}}) + (E_{2_{i,j}} - R_2(\mathbf{n}_{2_{i,j}}))R_2(\mathbf{n}_{2_{i,j}})$$
$$+ \lambda_1\mathbf{n}_{2_{i,j}}(\mathbf{n}_{1_{i,j}} \cdot \mathbf{n}_{2_{i,j}} - \cos(\theta)) + \lambda_2(\mathbf{n}_{1_{i,j}}\mathbf{n}_{2_{i,j}}\mathbf{Nc})(\mathbf{n}_{2_{i,j}} \times \mathbf{Nc})$$
$$-\mu_{1_{i,j}}\mathbf{n}_{1_{i,j}} = 0. \qquad (6.12)$$

From Equation 6.12, an iterative scheme may be derived:

$$\mathbf{n}_{1_{i,j}}^{(k+1)} = \frac{1}{\mu_{1_{i,j}}}[(E_{1_{i,j}} - R_1(\mathbf{n}_{1_{i,j}}^{(k)}))R_1'(\mathbf{n}_{1_{i,j}}^{(k)}) +$$
$$(E_{2_{i,j}} - R_2(\mathbf{n}_{2_{i,j}}^{(k)}))R_2'(\mathbf{n}_{2_{i,j}}^{(k)}) + \lambda_1\mathbf{n}_2^{(k)}(\mathbf{n}_1^{(k)} \cdot \mathbf{n}_2^{(k)} - \cos(\theta)) +$$
$$\lambda_2(\mathbf{n}_{2_{i,j}}^{(k)}\mathbf{n}_{1_{i,j}}^{(k)}\mathbf{Nc})(\mathbf{n}_{2_{i,j}}^{(k)} \times \mathbf{Nc})]. \qquad (6.13)$$

Now, note that $\frac{1}{\mu_{1_{i,j}}}$ does not change the direction of the vector being computed, thus we may eliminate the Lagrange multiplier and normalise the vector explicitly.

$$\mathbf{m}_{1_{i,j}}^{(k+1)} = (E_{1_{i,j}} - R_1(\mathbf{n}_{1_{i,j}}^{(k)}))R_1'(\mathbf{n}_{1_{i,j}}^{(k)}) + (E_{2_{i,j}} - R_2(\mathbf{n}_{2_{i,j}}^{(k)}))R_2'(\mathbf{n}_{2_{i,j}}^{(k)})$$
$$+\lambda_1\mathbf{n}_2^{(k)}(\mathbf{n}_1^{(k)} \cdot \mathbf{n}_2^{(k)} - \cos(\theta)) + \lambda_2(\mathbf{n}_{2_{i,j}}^{(k)}\mathbf{n}_{1_{i,j}}^{(k)}\mathbf{Nc})(\mathbf{n}_{2_{i,j}}^{(k)} \times \mathbf{Nc}), (6.14)$$

$$\mathbf{n}_{1_{i,j}}^{(k+1)} = \frac{\mathbf{m}_{1_{i,j}}^{(k+1)}}{\parallel \mathbf{m}_{1_{i,j}}^{(k+1)} \parallel}. \tag{6.15}$$

A similar derivation may be followed for $\mathbf{n}_{2_{i,j}}^{(k+1)}$.

In the case of a Lambertian reflectance model:

$$R(\mathbf{n}) = \mathbf{n} \cdot \mathbf{s}, R'(\mathbf{n}) = \mathbf{s}. \tag{6.16}$$

Equation (6.14) becomes:

$$\mathbf{m}_{1_{i,j}}^{(k+1)} = (E_{1_{i,j}} - \mathbf{n}_{1_{i,j}}^{(k)} \cdot \mathbf{s})\mathbf{s} + (E_{2_{i,j}} - \mathbf{n}_{2_{i,j}}^{(k)} \cdot \mathbf{s})\mathbf{s} +$$
$$\lambda_1 \mathbf{n}_2^{(k)}(\mathbf{n}_1^{(k)} \cdot \mathbf{n}_2^{(k)} - \cos(\theta)) + \lambda_2(\mathbf{n}_1^{(k)}\mathbf{n}_2^{(k)}\mathbf{Nc})(\mathbf{n}_{2_{i,j}}^{(k)} \times \mathbf{Nc}). \tag{6.17}$$

In the following cases there are boundary conditions to find a unique solution:

1	a discontinuity between two surfaces where the angle between the surfaces is known;	$\mathbf{n}_1 \cdot \mathbf{n}_2 = \cos\theta,$ $E_1 - R_1(\mathbf{n}_1) = 0,$ $E_2 - R_2(\mathbf{n}_2) = 0,$ $\mathbf{n}_1\mathbf{n}_2\mathbf{Nc} = 0.$
2	an occluding limb; and	$\mathbf{n} = \mathbf{Nc}.$
3	a singular point.	$\mathbf{n} = -\mathbf{s}$, (lambertian case).

In the case of occluding limbs, the surface normal may be set directly by calculating the normal to the tangent of the extracted edge. A singular point has only one possible solution to the irradiance equation, so the surface normal will be set directly. However, the three surface vertex case of Malik and Maydan need not be considered, as this is a sub-case of 1.

Once shape has been determined at the boundary it can be propagated shape across surfaces, using the variational technique of [24].

In some situations, noise in the image may cause distortions in shape estimates. In a typical solution to the shape-from-shading problem the use of a mean filter will result in the distortion of discontinuities in the image. However, using a knowledge-based approach, filtering and regularisation can be performed along each edge and surface separately as edge locations have already been found. This prevents the usual problems of distorting the solution away from the true surface. Edge preserving smoothing [99] would be another way of approaching this. However, edge-preserving smoothing techniques have known shortcomings, such as the loss of corners, and introduction of artifacts in neighbourhood operations.

6.4   Knowledge-based Implementation

This section describes a frame-based architecture that systematically applies a set of known facts, processes and rules for finding a unique solution for the object's shape. The method assumes as a starting point, that segmentation and labelling of the image have been performed by a model-based edge matching process, such as that described in the previous chapter.

There are three main types of knowledge used in this process, namely: facts, rules, and processes. The facts consist of correspondences between geometric structures of the object and perceived structures in the image, facts about properties of the object itself, and facts about the environment in which the image was taken. There may also be domain specific facts about the type of object being viewed. The rules include: knowledge of how to apply the facts and processes to solve the required problem; rules about how to proceed in cases of failure; and standard deductive rules to reach the goals of the system. The processes include: the image processing tasks required to perform shape-from-shading; and the know-how of how these are performed (e.g., finding boundary conditions before attempting to solve surfaces).

6.4.1   Knowledge / frame topology

For shape-from-shading, knowledge of an object is most naturally structured as it is perceived in the image, because the shape derivation process begins from a projected image. Canonical-views (as presented in Chapter 4) model the object. Within each model view of the object, surfaces and edges, and information about them, need to be represented. By modelling each canonical-view using a frame, the transition of the viewer from one viewpoint to another can be modelled as the transformation between a frame representing each view.

Our frame system consists of object, view, surface, and edge frames to represent objects. There is also a frame to handle environment information, in this case light source direction and albedo. An inten-

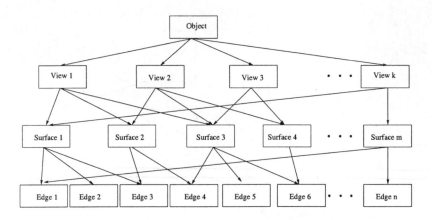

Figure 6.3: In our object representation, an object has several (possibly overlapping) views, each view has visible surfaces (views may overlap and so share common surfaces), and each surface will have some edges (surfaces will typically have some common edges).

sity image frame abstracts the interface to the image simplifying and safe-guarding the access required by the frames which perform the processing. Figure 6.3 shows the hierarchy of representation in the object frame structures. An object frame represents a single object, and has terminals, or subframes for each of the represented views of the object. Each view frame has terminals, or subframes consisting of surfaces and edges. Figure 6.4 shows an example of instantiated frames for a camera image of the guitar presented in an experiment in this chapter. The frame system was implemented in c++.

6.4.2   Fact knowledge

When an object is recognised, it is matched to one of the views of the object frame using the edge-based matching described in the previous chapter. Matching instantiates image features to all edges and surfaces within the view frame. If a frame fails to match sufficient slots, it is exchanged for a frame of a spatially neighbouring view, and matching is attempted again. View frames also store type descriptions for each edge. Surface frames contain a list of attached edges and their types for the current view which is passed to them by the instantiated view frame. They contain information about a reflectance model (this may be the same for all surfaces). Surface frames may also contain a descrip-

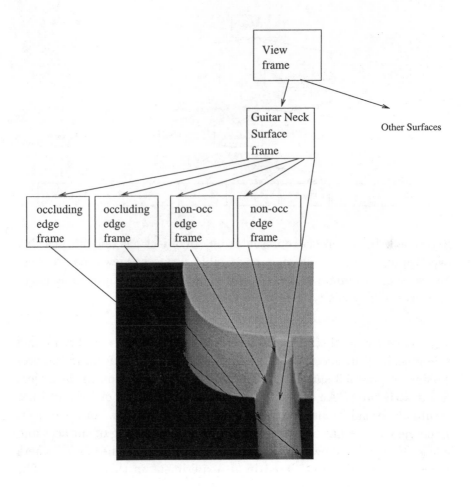

Figure 6.4: Instantiation of frames for the guitar image. There are five surfaces visible in this view. One of these is the guitar neck which has two occluding limb boundaries and two non-occluding edge boundary visible (other edges are modelled for this surface, but has no shape from shading calculations). The edge frames instantiate the edge pixel locations, and calculate shape at the corresponding image locations. The surface frame uses the instantiated edges to delimit the pixels it operates on. Note that the edge where the guitar neck joins the body on the right-hand side of the image is not modelled as part of it is a jump edge rather than an orientation discontinuity. It would be inaccurate to model it as either orientation discontinuity or as a limb-boundary.

tion of expected surface shape if the system was employed for model matching. Finally, they contain a normal needle map for the surface, which is a product of the process. The processing method presented treats occluding edges and orientation discontinuities differently, but a single edge subframe supports both types, as an edge may be occluding in one view, and an orientation discontinuity in another. The frames contain the pixel locations of the edges, which also delineate the surfaces in the image. For curved occluding edges, the tangent will be calculated at every point along the edge. For orientation discontinuities, the edge frame has a set of pixel locations for each surface. These are typically a few pixels away from the edge to avoid difficulties with narrow bands of high curvature. Orientation discontinuity edge frames also have a slot for the angle between the surface normals of the edges, in most cases this is a single value. However, for more complex surfaces this may be a function of position along the edge. If the edge is not curved and is occluding, only pixel location information is used.

6.4.3 Procedural knowledge

Procedural knowledge consists of the numeric processes that can be performed to find the shape of an object as well as the order and way in which they are performed, and the process of initialisation (setting terminal defaults). Note that initialisation may be domain specific. The numerical process has three parts: (1) Brooks and Horn's method [24] for propagating shape across surfaces given boundary conditions; (2) the new method, presented here, of calculating the surface normal along orientation discontinuities; and (3) the method of setting the surface normal along limb boundaries based on the tangent to the edge.

The required order of processing is to calculate normals for any solvable edges, then solve for surfaces, and finally combine this for the view. Also, before any object recognition shape matching can occur for a surface, all numeric shape processing must be complete for that surface. Similarly, all surfaces must have completed processing and matching before matching can occur for the view. Finally, default values for surface terminals can generally be set using surface direction based on estimates of object pose extracted during model matching, and the assumption of a flat surface. However, far better initialisation can be achieved in specific domains. This is discussed further in the results (see Figure 6.9).

6.4.4   Shape processing rulebase

The rulebase assumes that an edge matching process has instantiated a view frame to an image. Within the view frame, all surface and edge frames are instantiated to sets of pixel locations in the image. The rulebase shown in Table 6.1 is partitioned by the basic order of processing which is reflected in the frame structure. There may also be further domain specific rules.

6.5   Experimental Method and Results

These experiments demonstrate the efficacy of the knowledge-based approach to shape-from-shading. The output of these experiments is a surface normal map. 3D reconstruction is not justified as the exact shape of the object is not required. For object recognition, properties such as surface curvature can be estimated directly from surface normals, and an approximate estimate of protrusion of the surface beyond the edges can also be made based on the surface normals.

The algorithm was tested against synthetic images generated by the POV Ray ray tracing package to allow full verification of results compared to ground truth. It was also run against real images taken through a minitron javelin CCD camera, and from the ORL face database. The synthetic images were used both raw, and with varying amounts of Gaussian noise added.

The images used were:

- a synthetic sphere;

- a synthetic dodecahedron;

- a camera image of an egg;

- a camera image of a guitar; and

- face images from the ORL face database.

6.5.1   Synthetic images

Gaussian noise was generated with a signal to noise ratio based on the mean signal (intensity value) of the image. The figures shown in table 6.2 are measured in decibels: $10 \log_{10} \left(\frac{s}{n} \right)^2$.

Antecedent	Quantity
Object	
Process: OR view match succeeds	Object match found for current view
Process: OR view match fails	Match next closest neighbouring view
Process: OR view match fails no more to match	Object match fails.
Process: OR no evidence from view match	Match closest neighbouring view Reject only if another view match is found
View	
Process: OR No surfaces can calculate shape	No evidence.
Process: surface normal map No surfaces can calculate shape	No surface normals can be found
Process: OR Shape calculated for ≥ 1 surfaces, all of these are correct matches.	Correct match.
Process: OR Failed to match ≥ 1 surfaces	View match fails
Process: surface normal map Have normal map for ≥ 1 surfaces	Write normal map for extracted surfaces
Surface	
One or more boundary conditions	Calculate surface normals using Brooks and Horn's method
Process: OR Convergent surface solution	Derive surface properties and compare to expected ranges
Process: OR No boundary conditions available	No evidence for surface
Process: surface normal map No boundary conditions available	No normal map for surface
Process: OR Fails to converge	No evidence for surface
Process: surface normal map Fails to converge	No normal map for surface
Limb boundaries	
	Set surface normals at edge points normal to the edge
Orientation discontinuities	
	Apply new SFS algorithm.

Table 6.1: Knowledge-based shape-from-shading rule base for processes of Object Recognition (OR), or producing a surface normal map.

Figure 6.5 shows the method's performance for a synthetic sphere. This demonstrates that the algorithm is able to find the shape of a curved object with curved occluding boundaries automatically. The boundary normals are set without intervention based on the normal to the tangent of the occluding edge, assuming the location of the edge is found prior to this process. Figure 6.5 (c) shows the needle map extracted for the synthetic sphere of Figure 6.5 (a). The image with Gaussian noise added at a signal to noise ratio of 10db is shown in Figure 6.5 (b), and Figure 6.5 (d) shows the extracted surface normal map using a 9-point mean filter. For Figure 6.5 (a) with no noise, the error from ground truth is 9.1%. This high error is largely due to the digitisation errors in the shape of the edge resulting in an imperfect estimate of the surface normal at the occluding boundary. This error can be seen at the edge surface normals, particularly at the top. The performance could be improved somewhat by using a more accurate discrete approximation to the tangent than the 3-point estimate that was used for these experiments. The surface normal map for the sphere was initialised with all vectors being normal to the page, pointing out- wards, consistent with a flat surface.

Figure 6.6 shows the method's performance on a dodecahedron. In this case, there are no visible curved occluding boundaries or singular points. No existing variation-based methods the author has seen, nor that of Oliensis and Dupuis could produce surface normals without having to explicitly set boundary conditions. The noiseless image the error was 2.9%. The surface normal pattern still shows the shape of the object with the magnitude of the noise equal to the magnitude of the signal, The surfaces are still visibly planar as shown in Figure 6.6 (d), despite the image being quite distorted in 6.6 (b). The surfaces for the dodecahedron were initialised individually which is consistent with the knowledge-based approach. The leftmost surface was initialised to point to the left-hand side of the image, similarly, the rightmost surface was pointing to the right-hand side. The surface facing the viewer was pointing directly toward the viewer, and the upper surface was pointing straight up. In a typical case for a recognition system, these surfaces would be initialised based on an estimate of object orientation.

Table 6.2 shows the performance for the sphere and dodecahedron images with varying amounts of noise. The first column shows the performance using an 8-point mean, while the second column shows performance against the image using raw intensity values. The results show that although there is noticeable degradation of performance with

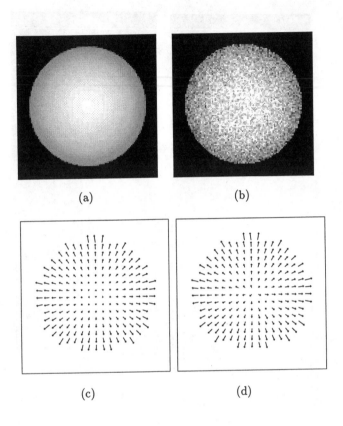

(a)   (b)

(c)   (d)

Figure 6.5: This figure shows the system's performance on a synthetic image of a sphere: (a) image without noise, (b) image with Gaussian noise of 10db SNR, (c) the surface normals calculated for the noiseless image, (d) the surface normals calculated for the noisy image.

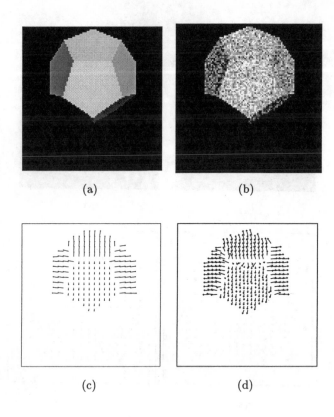

(a)   (b)

(c)   (d)

Figure 6.6: The system's performance on an image of a dodecahedron:
(a) Clean image, (b) Image with Gaussian noise added with a magnitude equal to the signal, (c) calculated surface normals for the clean
image, (d) calculated surface normals for the noisy image. The two
lower surfaces are ignored as too little surface area is shown to contribute much.

SNR Sphere	Error with mean	Error without mean
No noise	0.093	0.091
40 db	0.096	0.095
20 db	0.104	0.117
15 db	0.115	0.147
10 db	0.140	0.200
Dodecahedron		
No noise	0.040	0.029
40 db	0.040	0.030
20 db	0.045	0.045
15 db	0.051	0.062
10 db	0.069	0.100
0 db	0.159	0.255

Table 6.2: For the signal to noise ratio shown, after 1000 iterations the results were as shown in the third column. The second column shows the performance when a nine point mean filter is applied to the segmented surfaces as part of the knowledge-based shape extraction process.

the addition of noise, it is reasonably graceful. They also show that the mean filter gives a small negative effect for images with very low noise, but an increasingly positive effect with larger noise level. A 4-point mean filter was also trialled, the effect was similar, but less significant.

Throughout these tests the error figures stated are calculated as the average Euclidean distance between the calculated vector and ground truth, over all calculated surface normals of the object (background is discounted).

$$noise = \frac{\sum_{i=0}^{n} \sqrt{\Delta x_i^2 + \Delta y_i^2 + \Delta z_i^2}}{n}, \quad (6.18)$$

where n is all the vectors calculated from the object, and Δx, Δy, Δz are the differences between the values of the true surface normals against those calculated.

The use of a filter here may yield computation time advantages in the case where knowledge-based shape-from-shading is used to derive an approximate value, such as for object recognition. If only approximate shape is required, the calculation may be performed at lower resolution based on local means. This will not result in degradation of edges because the knowledge-based approach allows the application of a mean filter separately across surfaces, and along edges.

6.5.2   Real images

The images shown here are large (256*256), and as such, took thousands of iterations for Brooks and Horn's method to converge on the large surfaces. Horn's suggestion [105] of modifying the weight of the regularisation is utilised. The system begins with a large weight ($\lambda = 1.0$ in Equation (2.2) in Chapter 2) on regularisation. Once the solution has converged the regularisation component is reduced to a small value ($\lambda = 0.005$) so the method can converge to a more correct solution. The regularisation component is not removed entirely because it is not feasible to obtain an exact solution with real data [105].

Figure 6.7(b) shows the method's performance on an egg. The surface normal needle map can be seen to correspond approximately to the egg's shape.

Figure 6.8 shows the surface normals extraction from an image of a guitar. This demonstrates that the method is capable of deriving the shape of complex objects, with a combination of planar surfaces, occluding limb boundaries, and orientation discontinuities. However,

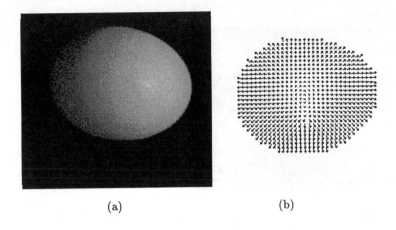

(a)   (b)

Figure 6.7: A camera image of an egg, and the surface normals extracted.

as the full boundary information for the surface cannot be inferred, some of the surfaces have not fully converged to the correct solution. With planar surfaces initialisation based on known edges ensures this is not a problem. However, for the large curving surface on the body of the guitar, in the region near the occluding non-limb boundary, the solution is not correct. Partial solutions in the case of incomplete boundary information is discussed in [115]. The partial information extracted can still be used by a knowledge-based system. It must be pointed out that most methods available in the literature would not be able to find this solution without additional knowledge as the occluding boundaries and singular points do not give enough shape constraints for a unique solution.

6.5.3 Domain knowledge

In this section the application of domain knowledge to aid in extracting the shape of objects is demonstrated. The examples given are images human faces. The ability to identify individual people is useful for robots that operate among people in office environments, especially if interaction with people is required. However, this experiment is also intended as an example of the general power of the use of domain knowledge. Human face images have complex shapes and non-uniform albedo. However, by using domain knowledge, the system can extract

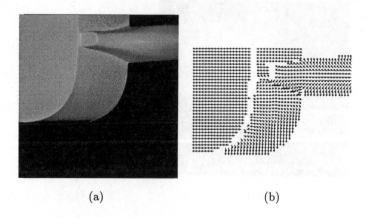

(a)   (b)

Figure 6.8: This figure shows a camera image of the back of a guitar which was painted matte white, and the shape extracted.

useful shape information from difficult images.

In the domain of face recognition, strong assumptions can be made about the underlying structure to help in extracting the shape of faces. For instance, the presence of a nose in the centre of the face, will be an appropriate assumption for frontal face images. Assumptions of this nature allow boundary conditions to be found, and can provide good initialisation of surface shape which could dramatically decrease the computational time required to find the shape of the face. To illustrate this point, experiments are presented based on two face images from the Olivetti and Oracle Research Laboratory database of faces (see http://www.cam-orl.co.uk/facedatabase.html). The surface normals at the boundaries of the face were set as occluding limb boundaries.[2] The surface normals for the faces were initialised to a convex ellipsoidal shape, which gives the shape-from-shading process a significant start. More complex models based on standard face shape, and boundary assumptions that are more generally applicable could clearly be applied.

Note that for these images, the final results are equivalent to those that would be given by Brooks and Horn [24] if boundary conditions were set by hand. The experiment demonstrates the advantages of domain-specific knowledge, and that this method can produce excellent

---

[2]Note this only fully bounds the face if there is little or no hair.

results from complex images with non-uniform albedo.

After only 200 iterations the solution converged. The normals changed on average by just 0.6% in the next 800 iterations. Given a flat surface as a starting point, and regularisation weight of 0.005, the solution was visibly incorrect after thousands of iterations. With a flat surface starting point, but with an initially high weight for regularisation, the solution also took thousands of iterations to converge.

6.6 Conclusion

This chapter presented a knowledge-based method for extracting the shape of an object from a single intensity image of an object when an edge match has been performed. This method allows the system presented in this book to differentiate objects on the basis of their shape as well as their edges. By using a knowledge-based approach the system is able to derive the shape for complex objects that are only piecewise smooth, and may have no limb boundaries or singular points. This chapter presented the derivation of a method for uniquely finding the shape along orientation discontinuities within the image, where the angle of the adjoining surfaces is known. This also demonstrates the efficacy of tackling shape-from-shading, and early vision processing tasks in general, with a knowledge-based approach and not entirely precognitively.

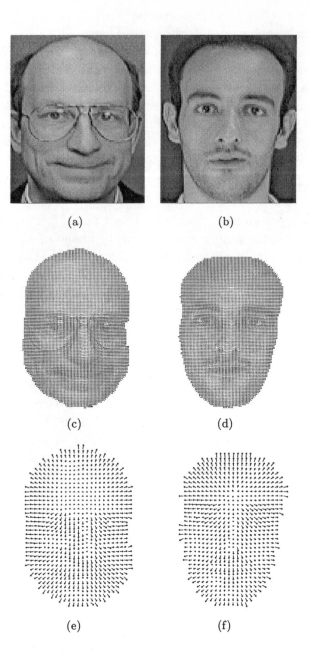

Figure 6.9: This figure shows two faces from the Olivetti and Oracle Research Laboratory database of faces (a-b), and surface normals derived from them. (c-d) show the derived normals of the faces with a high density of displayed points, while (e-f) show derived normals with a low density of displayed points.

Chapter 7

Supporting Navigation Components

This chapter describes aspects of the robot system that are essential to its operation. However, these aspects are not the key focus of this book. Specifically, Section 1 describes a path planning approach; and Section 2 discusses the interface with an odometry and obstacle detection system. The odometry and obstacle detection system was developed separately by others in our Laboratory. The work presented here is an original implementation with some original algorithms, but also incorporates the use of some well-known methods.

The path planning system is given an estimate of the relative object position, and forms a local path segment. The robot moves along this segment, avoiding any obstacles. See Figure 7.1 for the relation of this component to the other parts of the system.

7.1 Model-based Path Planning

To circumnavigate an object, a robot should follow the object surface normal, executing a path that is at a minimum safe distance from the object. Circumnavigation can be performed as a series of view-based local navigation problems. At each point, the robot's task is to move along the nearest surface in the direction of circumnavigation. To this end, the robot assesses the relative pose and position of the object, and the distance it should move, then calculates a local path, and follows

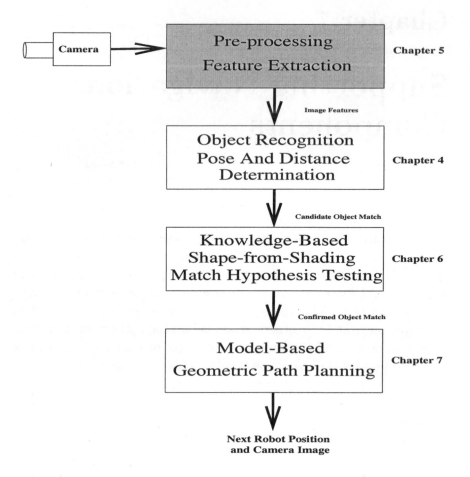

Figure 7.1: This chapter describes the path planning and navigation component of the system.

the path using odometry. The robot performs such local navigation tasks until the task is complete.

The robot should remain at a safe distance from the object to prevent collision. However, the actual distance is task dependent. For object inspection the robot may be required to remain close to the object. While for docking, the robot will be required to move in close to a particular point after navigating around the object. If the robot is close to the object it must move slowly and regularly check is position in order to allow for errors in object position estimates and odometry. If the robot is further away less caution is necessary. Other factors that must be considered in determining what is a suitable robot-to-object distance are motivated by object recognition and pose determination. The distance needs to be large enough to fit the object (or the part of the object that is modelled in the corresponding view) into the image for recognition, yet small enough for object points to be well spread in the image, allowing accurate pose and distance determination.

A one-dimensional variant on the idea of the distance transform [120] is applied for the robot to plan a path to a required object surfaces, such as is required for docking. The system can count the total number of surfaces that will be encountered in travelling from its initial position to the docking site in either direction. The system then chooses the direction which visits the least number of surfaces.

Implementation

A path around the object is planned *a priori* by expanding the boundaries of the object in two dimensions, similar to the *configuration space* approach [148]. The boundaries are expanded by an amount considered appropriate for the object and task. Figure 7.3 shows the path derived for the computer terminal used in previous work [12]. This is a continuous path of points where it is ideal for the robot to take images of the object to assess its relative position. A geometric method for planning the path around the object is used so that collision-free motion can be ensured. However, other planning methods could also be applied.

Given that processing an image to find the object location requires a finite time interval, the robot needs to move far enough based on an individual assessment to progress at a reasonable rate, preferably with continuous motion. However, it must not move so far that it is in danger of colliding with the object. The approach used was to move a distance based on the minimum of: (1) the estimated distance to the object, minus a safety threshold; and (2) the distance the robot moves in the time taken to process an image. Using (2), the robot will move continuously, if it is a large enough distance from the object, and every image is processed correctly. An appropriate odometric coordinate transform must be applied to the estimate of object position as the robot will have moved some distance since it grabbed an image of the object.

To circumnavigate based on the generated path the robot calculates the distance to move. It determines the closest object surface and checks if a circle centred at its current position, with the radius of the distance to move, intersects with the expanded object boundary of the nearest surface (see Figure 7.2). Otherwise, the robot checks if the circle intersects with the path around the corner which joins the nearest surface and the next surface on the path in the desired direction of robot motion. Checking continues until an intersection is found, then the robot moves in a straight line to this point. As the robot never moves further than the robot-to-object distance it may move in a straight line to its next destination. The robot will stay fairly close to the path provided that it generally moves most of the distance, or its moves are small in comparison with the path's curvature.

Clearly, this straight line approximation to the path, and the use of a configuration space approach will lead to a sub-optimal path, that may not be very smooth (the robot will turn and move, and sometimes pause to process when matches fail). Some improvements could be made in this area; however, this is not the emphasis of this book.

Note, that if a concavity in the object is encountered, the generated path remains at least the required distance from any surface at all times. Figure 7.3 shows a computer terminal that was circumnavigated in an early simulated trial. Between points (3) and (4), the path does not run all the way around to be perpendicular to the small surface behind the screen. To do so would bring the path too close to the adjoining edge, which is similar for position (9).

Deriving expanded boundaries for surfaces

Object surfaces are modelled by planar faces and piecewise quadric surfaces. Planar surfaces are represented as a list of connected boundary points. The points making up the widest projected edge or edges in the plane of robot motion are expanded by taking the normal to the surface at each point c. This is done by taking the cross-product of

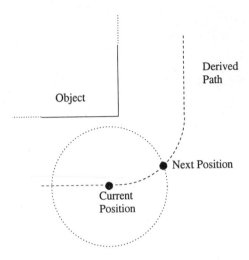

Figure 7.2: The robot calculates the distance to move and checks if a circle of that radius intersects with the expanded boundary of the nearest surface. If it does not intersect, the robot checks if the circle intersects with the path around the corner joining to the next surface as shown.

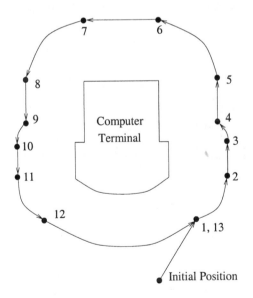

Figure 7.3: The circumnavigation path derived for a computer terminal.

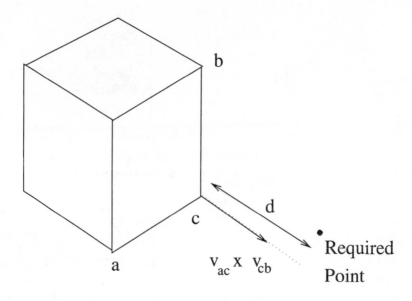

Figure 7.4: The vector cross product of three points determines the normal.

vectors from two other points in the plane a, b to c:

$$\vec{v}_{ac} \times \vec{v}_{cb},$$

and projecting it into the plane, and normalising:

$$(\hat{x} = \frac{x}{\sqrt{x^2 + y^2}}, \hat{y} = \frac{y}{\sqrt{x^2 + y^2}}, \hat{z} = 0)$$

For the point $c, (x_c, y_c)$, the projected point at the required distance d is:

$$(x_c + d\hat{x}, y_c + d\hat{y}),$$

where d is the required distance from the object. The points are joined with a straight line to form the extended boundary.

Elliptical surfaces are represented as a centre point (x_c, y_c, z_c), and radii in $(x, y, z), (a, b, c)$. Only convex non-rotated ellipsoids are handled.

$$\frac{(x + x_c)^2}{a^2} + \frac{(y + y_c)^2}{b^2} + \frac{(z + z_c)^2}{c^2} = 1$$

Figure 7.5 shows that the expanded ellipsoid is formed by expanding each radius by d:

$$\frac{(x + x_c)^2}{(a + d)^2} + \frac{(y + y_c)^2}{(b + d)^2} + \frac{(z + z_c)^2}{(c + d)^2} = 1$$

Note that this is only an approximation. The path will not be exactly at distance d from the ellipse at all times.

The widest extent of the ellipsoid in the plane is at the intersection of the ellipsoid, and the plane in x, y for the minimum absolute value of Z, z_{min}:

$$\frac{(x + x_c)^2}{(a + d)^2} + \frac{(y + y_c)^2}{(b + d)^2} + \frac{(z_{min} + z_c)^2}{(c + d)^2} = 1$$

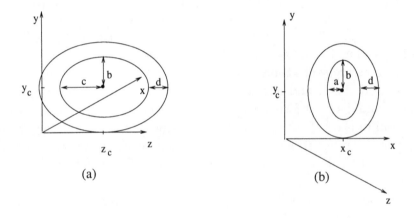

Figure 7.5: The expanded ellipsoid.

Corners arcs between adjacent surfaces are formed by taking the projected points for the corner on the two surfaces and joining them with an arc with a radius d, see the corners in Figure 7.3.

Finally, any lines which are subsumed by other lines or set of lines (closer to the object) are discarded. In Figure 7.3, note that the two short, collinear boundaries, behind the curved front surface (screen) have been subsumed between points 5 and 6. Any lines which intersect are cut at the intersection, as can be seen in Figure 7.3 where the arc (3)-(4) joins edge (4)-(5).

7.1.1   Path planning and obstacle avoidance

The discussion presented above assumes no obstacles block the robot's path. The system takes a reactive approach to obstacle avoidance to allow for some restricted dynamic motion in the environment. The robot still generates the ideal path *a priori* as described above, but before any move is made, the robot checks its path for obstacles.

7.2   Odometry and Obstacle Avoidance Subsystem

Object recognition and path planning are performed by a separate processor that communicates to the robot via a serial line. The robot has its own processor to handle odometry, robot motion control, and obstacle detection. The two processors communicate using simple commands: MOVE, TURN, PANLOCK, GETSTATUS, and OBSCHECK. The system diagram showing the interaction of these subsystems is shown in Figure 7.6. The communication protocol used is ASCII based, and uses short fixed length packets and simple error detection. As only a few bytes are sent at any time, speed is not a consideration.

The odometry and obstacle detection subsystem was developed by others, and does not form part of this book. The subsystem is described in detail in [112]. It uses an additional camera that is mounted on the front of the robot to look for obstacles that block the robot's forward path. Only the interface to the odometry and obstacle detection system is presented here.

The odometry and obstacle detection subsystem monitors robot position and orientation. The parameters for the robot control commands are shown in Table 7.2. The robot starting location is the origin of the odometric coordinate system.

Notes:

- The PANLOCK command locks the pan head onto the odometric coordinate specified. This is performed using closed loop control which is performed on the robot to avoid communication overhead.

- Only the GETSTATUS and OBSCHECK commands return values, all other commands are unacknowledged. GETSTATUS returns the current (x, y, θ) and θ_p, the current angle of rotation

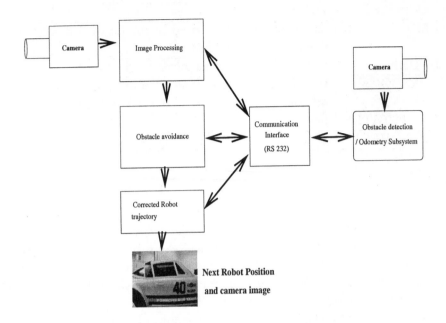

Figure 7.6: The interaction between the navigation and odometry/obstacle avoidance subsystems. The subsystems communicate via RS232. The position is checked when the image is first taken, as the robot moves a finite distance while processing. Before the robot path is changed, the path is checked for obstacles. If all is clear, the robot then alters its path.

of the pan platform, in odometric coordinates. GETSTATUS is used to monitor the current robot position, and monitor the progress of the other commands. OBSCHECK is described in the following section.

- During turns, the pan platform moves constantly to track the object. This leads to substantial vibration in the camera image due to the unsophisticated pan hardware. Thus, images are only acquired while the robot is either performing a MOVE or stopped.

7.2.1   Obstacle avoidance strategies

The OBSCHECK command is passed three parameters (see Figure 7.8) to check the path for obstacles for each proposed local path segment. An obstacle avoidance example is included in Chapter 8 to demonstrate

Command	Parameters
MOVE	the distance to be moved in the forward direction from the current location.
TURN	the rotation from the current orientation.
PANLOCK	the location in the plane of robot motion in odometric coordinates that the camera will track.
GETSTATUS	none.
OBSCHECK	ψ, ω, and ρ (Defined in Figure 7.8).

Figure 7.7: Robot commands and parameters.

that the approach is flexible enough to react to unanticipated events. A simple approach to obstacle avoidance was taken, based on the assumption that an obstacle will completely block the path of the robot. If an obstacle is detected that blocks the path, the robot will turn around and move around the object in the other direction towards the goal location. Clearly, more sophisticated approaches such as moving closer to the object to get around the obstacle are also possible.

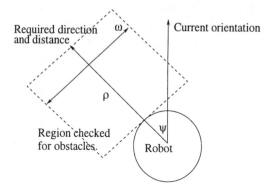

Figure 7.8: The obstacle detection subsystem checks a region around the desired path for obstacles. In this case, the robot checks in direction ψ, for a distance ρ, and width ω.

If the amount the robot turns is small enough to allow it to check the required path for obstacles, it will do so before it performs the turn. Otherwise, it will turn first then check the requested move. The robot used in experiments for this book performs turns in place, and so turns cannot lead directly to collisions.

7.2.2 Coordinate transforms

The robot's estimate of object location and required destination point are initially in camera-centred coordinates. Further, the image used to determine the relative object position is taken while the robot is moving. Let $(x^{im}, y^{im}, \theta^i m)$ be the odometric position at the time the image is taken, and let the robot's final position be (x^f, y^f, θ^f). The robot's estimated destination point and the object location are relative to (x^{im}, y^{im}). We can derive a transform, Γ, from camera-centred coordinates to odometric coordinates, with an additional offset between the final robot position in odometric coordinates (x^f, y^f) and (x^{im}, y^{im}).

Γ is applied to both the destination coordinates and the object location. The destination coordinates are finally transformed back into robot-centred polar coordinates to calculate the parameters of the TURN and MOVE commands. The transformed object location coordinates are passed as parameters to PANLOCK.

Chapter 8

Fuzzy Control for Active Perceptual Docking

The robot is engaged in a docking manœuvre guided by an active perceptual behaviour. In order to dock with an object, the robot must control its heading direction to move directly towards the object. In previous work, we developed a technique in which the robot fixates on the desired target, and corrects its heading direction based on information derived from optical flow data from a log-polar camera. However, the optical flow data derived is noisy. Thus, when the robot direction control is based directly on the optical flow data the resulting path is erratic (see Figure 8.4 in the results section of this chapter). A smooth path is desirable as it reduces strain on motors and simplifies fixation. Furthermore, constant change in direction can result in wheel-slippage, leading to errors in odometry. High quality odometric information is of great advantage for position estimation in mobile robot navigation. Traditional control techniques are not effective in such situations, as it is almost impossible to establish precise models for optical flow data.

In this chapter, we use fuzzy control for mobile robot motion control based on visual perception, in particular, illustrate the application of fuzzy control for the docking problem, and demonstrate that fuzzy control leads to significantly smoother paths in simulation.

8.1 Introduction

This chapter presents an approach for mobile robot motion control using a fuzzy controller. We discuss general aspects of the selection of appropriate control models for mobile robot navigation, and why fuzzy control is chosen for mobile robot motion in some situations. We make use of the TSK (Takagi-Sugeno-Kang) fuzzy model, as described in [209, 213], to smooth the path of a mobile robot during a docking manœuvre.

The major aim of using fuzzy control in this chapter is to produce a smooth path for the robot in docking, while not impacting unduly the time for docking. A smooth path is important because it:

- simplifies fixation;

- reduces motor wear; and,

- improves odometric data.

Fixation adjusts a pan-tilt platform on the robot, to ensure the object remains centred in the camera at all times. If the robot undergoes a large rotational acceleration, the pan-tilt platform may need to undergo an even larger acceleration to compensate both for that of the robot, and the robot's translation. If there is no feedback from the robot drive system to the pan-tilt controller, fixation must be performed purely on visual data. Processing visual data quickly enough to keep up with large rotational accelerations can be problematic, and is better avoided.

Large accelerations should be restricted as they are taxing on motors, and the mechanical base of the robot. Finally, many mobile robot systems make use of odometric information from wheel encoders to track the robot position over time. A major source of odometric error arises from wheel slippage. Large accelerations cause slippage, particularly rotational accelerations where the robot is turning in one direction, and then suddenly reversed. So for accurate robotic navigation, it is important for the robot to follow a smooth path.

However, the robot's task is docking, so the requirement of a smooth path must be balanced with ensuring that the robot does not spend too much time travelling in the wrong direction.

8.1.1 Fuzzy control

As with any other systems, in order to control the motion of the robot, it is necessary to establish a mode based on the observed dynamic characteristics of the robot, and devise a control scheme such that the robot can be controlled by adjusting the control signal based on the monitored sensor output [166]. In traditional control theory, the control scheme is closely related to the precise mathematical model of the system and a set of well-defined objectives of what the control scheme is to achieve. The process of deriving a control scheme is that of mathematical optimisation. In general, the traditional control technique requires that:

1. the model of the system is known;

2. the objective function can be formulated in *precise* terms; and,

3. the optimisation problem can be solved.

Modern control theory has been well-established for more than 50 years since Wiener's seminal work on cybernetics in the mid 40's and Kalman's work on state-space approach to system optimisation and control in the mid 60's. Although, the modern control theory has enjoyed great success in many applications and was responsible for the Apollo Project, it has been limited only to cases where precise mathematical models can be established which are often extremely difficult to obtain. As a result, many control systems cannot perform robustly and collapse when the mathematical model does not reflect the reality.

Fuzzy control can be used in cases where traditional control fails [132]. In the early 70's fuzzy logic was successfully applied to such non-linear dynamic systems as steam generators [7] and cement plants [153], which are difficult to model let alone control robustly. Mamdani's linguistic model led to many significant developments in fuzzy control theory and applications. A particularly important model was developed by Takagi, Sugeno, and Kang [209, 213]. TSK fuzzy model is able to approximate non-linear systems from input-output data. Many researchers have used the TSK model in real-world applications and studied its properties, especially, stability and observer design [216]. Recently, Piegat has given an excellent treatment of the theories and applications of fuzzy modelling and control. Interested readers may consult this book for more details [180].

Fuzzy control allows the identification of the system either by [175]:

- knowledge acquisition from an expert to give fuzzy control rules; or,

- black-box identification via use of techniques such as clustering, neural nets, and genetic algorithms.

8.1.2   Fuzzy control for mobile robot control

In mobile robot control, sensor measurements are frequently noisy. The
noise in direct sensor outputs is quite well understood and can be modelled. However, the situation is more difficult for sensors such as vision
where a model of the world is required and complex algorithms may be
used to interpret the raw sensor data before it is used for robot control.
Vision systems for complex problems are generally custom-made. Significant work would be required to model the noise introduced at each
stage of the process. Even if this work is completed, deriving accurate
models of how noise aggregates between the components of the system
is a difficult problem.

Further, in all but the simplest cases, a mobile robot is dealing with
an environment that is only partially known, or completely unknown.
The environment may also be changing dynamically in unknown ways.
Thus, a precise model of the system is not possible in many cases.
In view of these facts, the noise in the final system outputs can be
non-Gaussian and non-stationary. We give two examples below.

For the direction control system presented in this chapter, all that
is known about the environment is that: the docking target object
is fixated by the camera; and, the majority of points in a given part
of the image are either behind or in front-of the fixated object. The
relative distances are unknown as is the distance from the target, which
is changing over time. In addition, the environment may be dynamic.
As we shall see in later sections, the relative distance has a direct
effect on the magnitude of the optical flow. To further complicate the
matter, our method for calculating optical flow without a model and
within a fast control loop involves a significant amount of noise. With
these problems, deriving a precise mathematical model appears to be
difficult.

In the case of the circumnavigation system described in this book,
the model of the object is known, and the best path for the robot
to take is well-defined. However, the object recognition component
of the system is complex. From the camera image, edges are taken,
these edges are joined, then matched to a model, and finally, based on
point correspondences, the position is estimated and a path generated.
Several types of error can occur:

- the system can fail to match at all;

- the system may match the object but the wrong surface in the model;

- the system may find a match in the background, which is un-known; or,

- the system may have the correct match, but the point identifica-tion is inaccurate, leading to an incorrect estimate of the object's position.

Finding precise mathematical models for such errors and system behaviour is difficult because the effects of the these errors do not follow some well-defined statistical models, e.g., the Gaussian model. Also, it is not always possible to identify which type of error has occurred. In the literature, researchers have used the Extended Kalman Filter [66, 234] to track odometry error, but they assume that localisation errors (corresponding to recognition is this system) can be modelled, however, this cannot be applied to the control of our mobile robot.

However, it is possible to provide an approximate linguistic descrip-tion of how the robot should behave. Similar problems exist for a wide variety of sensor-based mobile robot systems; particularly those in dy-namic, partially known, or unknown environments where sensor data processing software is complex. In such cases fuzzy control can be useful.

8.1.3   TSK fuzzy model

Takagi and Sugeno [213] proposed the T-S fuzzy model, and a proce-dure to identify the T-S model from input/output data of a system. This method was extended by Sugeno and Kang [209] in the S-K fuzzy model, as described also in [217]. The method consists of structure identification and parameter identification.

The TSK fuzzy model consists of a set of implication rules whose consequent parts are represented by linear equations as follows, If x_1 is A_{i1}, ..., x_k is A_{ik} THEN

$$y_i = p_{i0} + p_{i1}x_1 + ... + p_{ik}x_k, \qquad (8.1)$$

where p_{ij}, are consequent parameters, y_i is the output from the rule, and A_{ij} is a fuzzy set, $j \in (1,..k)$, and $i \in (1,..n)$, n is the number of rules, and k is the number of input variables.

Given an input $(x_1, x_2, ...x_k)$, the final output of the n implications of the fuzzy model is inferred as

$$y = \frac{\sum_{i=1}^{l} w_i y_i}{\sum_{i=1}^{l} w_i}, \tag{8.2}$$

where w_i is the weight of the ith IF-THEN rule for the input and is calculated as

$$w_i = A_{i1}(x_1) \wedge ... \wedge A_{ik}(x_k) \tag{8.3}$$

Different definitions of $\wedge$ are possible; for instance, Tanaka and Sugeno [217] define the w_i as

$$w_i = \prod_{k=1}^{n} A_{ik}(x_k), \tag{8.4}$$

where $A_{ik}(x_k)$ is the grade of membership of x_k in A_{ik}.

Fuzzy controller

To construct a TSK fuzzy controller requires the following:

1. Select premise variables, x_i (premise structure identification);

2. Partition input space for each rule, A_{ij} (premise structure identification);

3. Select the output variables, w_i (consequent structure identification);

4. Optimise fuzzy membership functions, A_i(premise parameter identification); and,

5. Optimise the consequent parameters, p_{ij} (consequent parameter identification).

Structure Identification

Identifying premise structure requires selecting the premise variables $(x_1, ..., x_k)$, and finding an optimal fuzzy partition of the input space $(A_{i1}, ..., A_{ik})$ for each rule. The purpose is to partition inputs into the fewest possible fuzzy subspaces that give adequate input space coverage. Too many fuzzy subspaces makes the model oversensitive to changes in the data used for structure identification. The consequent structure identification only requires selecting consequent variables.

Consequent Parameter Identification

Takagi and Sugeno use the root mean square of output errors as a performance index to optimise the consequence parameters. Define β_i as

$$\beta_i = \frac{A_{i1}(x_1) \wedge ... \wedge A_{ik}(x_k)}{\sum_{i=1}^{k}(A_{i1}(x_1) \wedge ... \wedge A_{ik}(x_k))} \tag{8.5}$$

then

$$y = \sum_{i=1}^{k} \beta_i(p_{i0}+p_{i1}.x_1+...+p_{ik}.x_k) = \sum_{i=1}^{k}(p_{i0}.\beta_i+p_{i1}.x_1.\beta_i+...+p_{ik}.x_k.\beta_i) \tag{8.6}$$

Thus, we can apply least squares to Equation (8.6) to obtain the parameter vector $P = (p_{i1}, ..., p_{ik})$ using a set of input-output data. Various other techniques are also possible to derive consequent parameters, for instance a neural net can be used to derive non-linear functions for the consequent parameters (e.g., [96]).

Each fuzzy set in the premises is determined by two parameters that give greatest grade 1 and least grade 0, as the membership functions are assumed to be linear. Takagi and Sugeno use complex method for the minimisation to find the optimal parameters of the fuzzy membership functions. In this chapter, we simply used gradient descent, which assumes the starting configuration set up by expert knowledge is close to the optimal solution.

8.1.4 Visual motion-based approaches to mobile robots and the docking problem

In order to be autonomous, it is necessary that the mobile robot perceive and react to its environment. A control system is required to take the sensory inputs (that are generally noisy) and produce smooth paths reducing motor wear and increasing odometric accuracy. Visual-guided motion-based approaches which use parameters derived from optical flow [15] as their control input variables are becoming increasingly popular in mobile robot navigation, for example [161, 192, 195, 193, 222]. This method develops a series of visual behaviours [194] which control the robot through a particular aspect of its task. The behaviour-based approach [83] uses a collection of such behaviours to solve complex robotic tasks.

However, the computation of optical flow without the use of models in environments where light is not carefully controlled often suffers from noise. The problem is more severe for effective real-time mobile robot navigation. Thus, it is important to examine possible control strategies for these systems to generate efficient paths from noisy input.

The control system presented in this chapter is for heading direction control in docking. Docking is a fundamental problem in mobile robot research. A robot must be able to dock in order to interact with objects in its environment. Thus, for operations such as manipulation (e.g., autonomous fork-lifts [82]), or industrial assembly [144, 102], the mobile robot must perform docking.

Section 8.2 describes the details of the mobile robot problem that requires a fuzzy control system. Section 8.3 describes the fuzzy control scheme for this system. Finally, Section 8.4 shows the results of the fuzzy control scheme in comparison with the use of the raw signal.

8.2   Direction Control for Robot Docking

This section describes a method for mobile robot guidance that uses data derived from the log-polar optical flow resulting from the motion field around a fixated object.

8.2.1   The log-polar camera

The log-polar sensor is a foveated sensor, in which sensing elements appear in a non-uniform distribution, with high density at the fovea that decreases continuously toward the periphery, see Figure 8.1. Mathematically, the transformation from the retinal plane in polar coordinates (ρ, θ) to log-polar Cartesian coordinates (ξ, γ) in the cortical plane can be expressed as follows,

$$\xi = log_a \frac{\rho}{\rho_0}, \tag{8.7}$$

$$\gamma = q\eta, \tag{8.8}$$

where (ρ, η) are the polar coordinates of a point on the retinal plane ρ_0, and q and a are constants determined by the sensor's physical layout.

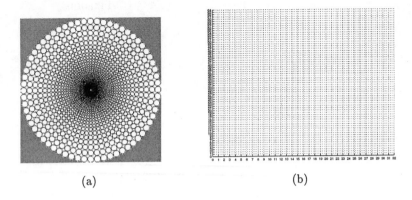

(a)   (b)

Figure 8.1: The log-polar sensor samples at 64 evenly spaced angles around the sensor, at 32 radii. The sensing elements are increasingly large toward the periphery. (a) The sensor geometry. (b) The image geometry.

8.2.2   Docking for a ground-based robot

Consider a ground-based robot, moving with a velocity $\mathbf{W} = (W_x, W_z)$ (Figure 8.2). The robot has a pan/tilt platform that is fixating on an object of interest using some method for fixation such as [92], [91], or [18]. The platform has rotational velocities of θ and ϕ for pan and tilt respectively. The platform has no capacity for rotation about the optic axis. Assume, without loss of generality, that the target object lies along the z axis, where the origin is fixed to the robot along the camera optical axis.

In order for the robot to dock with the target object, it must adjust its heading direction so that W_x is reduced to zero. We do not consider the problem of controlling the magnitude of velocity, which has been addressed previously (e.g., [184, 222]). The method can handle the case where the direction control is independent of the fixation process, and the pan angle is unknown.

In the region at the top and bottom of the sensor, where $cos\frac{\gamma}{q}$ is maximal, the equation for the rotational component of image velocity in the log polar sensor can be approximated as follows. (See [13] for a full derivation.)

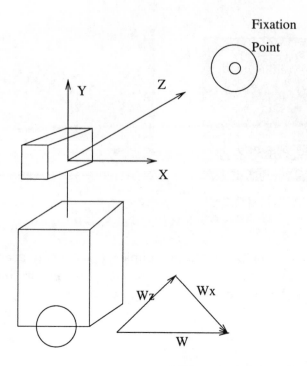

Figure 8.2: The robot moves on the ground plane, while the camera fixates on a point in the environment.

$$\dot{\gamma} = \frac{qF}{\rho D}(\frac{D}{Z} - 1)W_x sin\frac{\gamma}{q},\qquad(8.9)$$

where D is the distance to the point of fixation.

In many situations, we may have knowledge of the depth of visible points in the camera image from the context of a robot's operation. In this docking scenario, we are interested in the depth of points relative to the camera fixation point. For example, when the fixation point is on the ground, all image points below it are ground points that are closer to the robot than the fixation point, and the majority of points above the object are background, and so more distant than the fixation point. (This assumes the space between the object and the robot is not cluttered with other objects).

Thus, we know the sign of the relative depth, and therefore the sign of $\dot{\gamma}$ with respect to W_x for some fraction of pixels in the image.

8.2.3   Noise in the input parameter

There are two major sources of noise in this system. They arise from noise in the flow calculation, and as a result of the unknown environment. The optical flow method used in this system [228] was selected because it did not require a model of the scene, and was fast. However, the flow data generated is noisy. See [15, 117] for extensive discussion of optical flow and the performance of optical flow methods. The environment also introduces noise that means that prevents us from knowing the relation between the magnitude of the flow and the magnitude of W_x. Equation 8.9 shows that the flow at any point depends on the ratio $\frac{D}{Z}$. However, we only know that, in general, the points in a particular region are close than, or further than the fixation point. Thus, we know only whether $\frac{D}{Z}$ is greater than or less than zero, not its magnitude. Knowledge that points are behind or in-front of the fixation point can often be derived from the context of what the robot is fixating on, and then general layout of the environment. However, the magnitude of these distances can only be estimated with a precise scene model, and precise knowledge of robot position and camera direction. With this knowledge, vision-based docking would be unnecessary, as the robot could move directly to the target.

Further, even if we knew the distribution of the noise introduced by the flow method, the fact that we do not know the magnitude of the flow at any particular point, means that the signal-to-noise ratio is unknown. We know that if a scene point is close to the fixation point then the signal will be small, and that if it is far, the signal will be large. If the fixation point is on an object that is far away in relation to the size of the object, then all points on that object will be close to the fixation point.

Also, for a particular point in the image, the distance may change rapidly as occluding objects move in and out of view. Without detailed knowledge of the environment, it is difficult to characterise all these factors mathematically. Finally, the position of the target relative to the robot is changing over time, and so it is not practical to estimate its true position by narrowing it down by combining multiple estimates as to whether it is to the left or right of the heading direction.

8.3   A Fuzzy Control Scheme

To derive a fuzzy control scheme, we collected data from a series of runs of the mobile robot in docking. This data includes the aggregated output from the optical flow data for each frame as the robot moved, $\sum \dot{\gamma}$, and the desired robot direction at this point, $\delta\theta$. There are up to 100 frames for each run, and several runs which took place under different conditions and with varying environments.

The only external input to the system is the optical flow data for each frame. Since in this system we assume that the target is stationary, it can expected that the sign of W_x will not change rapidly (until the system has converged). Thus, recursive information about which way we adjusted the heading direction last time is useful. Due to the noise in the optical flow, the optical flow information from the previous frame may be useful to ease the effect of the occasional poor frame. However, this can be adequately represented as a factor contributing to the state variable of the previous output. The only output is the adjustment to the heading direction. Thus, two input variables and an output variable have been identified.

In general,

- if the aggregate of the flow over the region of interest in the image is negative, then the robot should turn to the left;

- if the aggregate of the flow over the region of interest is positive, the robot should turn to the right; or

- if the aggregate of the flow over the region of interest is zero, the robot should continue in our present direction.

The rules derived that describe the desired behaviour are summarised in Table 8.1.

Our system originally included a positive low and a negative low membership function for the aggregates. Analysis of the training data found that this added no discriminating power to the controller, and so was collapsed to a single classification of zero. This can be understood by considering that, for small aggregate flow values, the noise resulting from the flow calculation is of a similar magnitude to the signal, thus negative low and positive low are both simply regarded as low.

There is little to be gained from a more extensive breakdown of the input aggregate flow variables. An aggregate of high magnitude

Current Aggregate	State	Output
Negative	Left	Left
Positive	Right	Right
Positive	Left	Zero
Negative	Right	Zero
Zero	Right	Small right
Zero	Left	Small left
Positive	Zero	Right
Negative	Zero	Left
Zero	Zero	Zero

Table 8.1: Fuzzy rules for docking control.

increases the certainty that it is a true indication of the sign of W_x. If the total signal is low, then the magnitude may be low, and noise will have a greater input, whereas large magnitude is likely to mean a large signal, and so noise is less likely to reverse the sign. However, a high magnitude of the aggregate does not necessarily indicate that the magnitude of W_x is large. If the points in the region of interest are far from the fixation point, we may get a large aggregate magnitude with a small value of W_x. Note, also that the distribution of points may change over time, particularly when the robot is turning, for example, if a background object moves into the field of view.

The membership functions for the input variables were optimised using sample data. We used gradient descent based on the root mean square of the output errors, see Equation 8.6. The resulting membership functions are shown in Figure 8.3.

8.4 Results

We present results of the control system using simulation. The results show that the control system smooths the path, preventing large accelerations, and that the total amount of time spent going in the wrong direction is not greatly impacted. We present four separate runs of the simulator. Each run includes around 30 iterations of the control system. By changing the control system in a closed loop, we modify the path that the robot will take. Thus, the results do not show a frame by frame comparison.

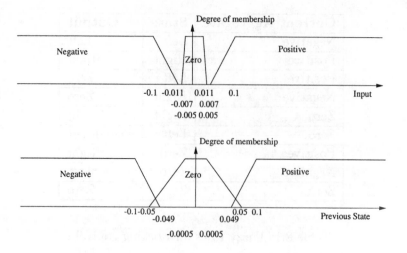

Figure 8.3: Fuzzy membership functions for the input variables: (a) rotational component of the optical flow, (b) previous state.

The robot simulator makes use of the POVRAY ray-tracing package for generating images. It simulates a robot that takes an image every p msec. The robot moves forward with a fixed velocity. The heading direction can be changed by applying angular velocity. This is represented as a mean velocity value over the p msec, representing that given the ramp up and ramp down of acceleration, the average velocity of v will lead to ap radians over the interval between images. The value of a is set by the control system.

There were four total trials to be compared. In the first trial the robot began heading 45° to the left of the target. The second trial had the same starting point, but began going 45° to the right of the target. The third trial began with the robot approximately 4% further back, and heading 45° to the left of the target, with the fourth trial beginning from the same point and moving to the right.

Figure 8.4 shows the heading direction angle over time, where zero is heading directly towards the target. This clearly shows that the change in angle is greatly smoothed, with some of the brief periods of turning in the wrong direction completely suppressed. For example, in (b) compare path the two negative paths between time intervals 9 and 13. Note that the control system cannot prevent extended periods of motion in the wrong direction due to an incorrect signal, but can only suppress noise spikes.

Figure 8.5 shows the path taken by the robot in each of the trial runs showing the difference of applying fuzzy control, and using the optical flow aggregate raw values. It shows that the fuzzy control system does not impede the convergence of the system, in fact in the negative cases an improvement in the convergence is evident. In the positive cases there is little apparent difference in the convergence. This shows a slightly smoother path with the control system in place. Note that because the paths taken with and without the control system are different, the images will be different, and so the input optical flow is different.

Figure 8.6 shows the comparative statistics across all trials of mean change in heading direction and maximum change in rotational velocity, for the periods shown in the graphs above.

The mean change in rotational velocity is reduced by almost half when the fuzzy controller is used. There are two principle reasons for this. Firstly, the raw outputs typically move from positive maximum (0.003) to negative maximum (-0.003) whenever the mean rotational velocity changes from a negative to a positive input (or vice versa). The control system will move at most from ±0.003 to zero. Secondly, we have introduced a fuzzy category of zero for the control system to allow for the uncertainty in the input. Thus, if the input value is close to zero, the control system will only alter slightly from its current heading direction. Thus, noisy values that fall close to zero will be largely suppressed in the fuzzy control system whereas otherwise they may have lead to a complete change direction.

The first aspect of the results could be introduced by any control system that uses hysteresis, so if we just set the rule that given negative direction, if we get one positive input we reduce rotational velocity to zero, then with a positive value, the output is set to positive. The second aspect of the rule is introduced with a fuzzy category of zero. Another method for defining a minimum threshold could be used, along with hysteresis, but this would be equivalent to the fuzzy controller shown here.

8.5 Conclusion

We have implemented a fuzzy control system to smooth the path of a mobile robot that is guided by the rotational component of log-polar optical flow in controlling its heading direction to dock with a fixated object. Our results demonstrate that the control system can smooth the path and prevent the robot turning too rapidly, easing stress on the motors and making odometry more reliable.

Fuzzy control has shown to be beneficial for controlling the path of a vision-guided mobile robot. In this case, traditional control systems were not appropriate as the system cannot be modelled mathematically with accuracy. Fuzzy control may be useful also for many other cases with vision-guided mobile robots, where the system cannot be accurately modelled.

Note that changing the control system for this application changes the performance of the final system, and so has an impact on the visual data that is used as an input. This can be seen from the examples in this chapter when the robot is approximately heading in the direction of the target. Unless the optical flow goes to zero, the control based on raw signal will continue oscillating, whereas ideally the control system should allow convergence. This means that it is difficult to obtain training data for the convergence case. We may use reinforcement learning to help the system explore the convergence part of the learning space. The use of reinforcement learning for fuzzy control vision-guided systems is an interesting area for further research.

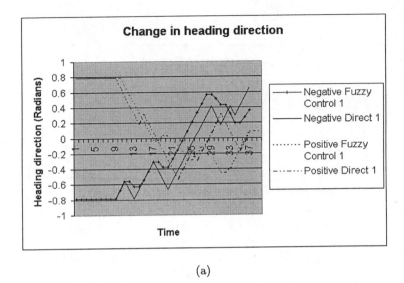

(a)

(b)

Figure 8.4: The heading direction of the simulated robot with respect to the target object. On the legend: Negative shows starting with a negative angle heading direction; Positive shows starting with a positive angle heading direction; Direct shows where the system used the truncated values directly from optical flow; and, Fuzzy Control shows that the fuzzy control system mediated the values. (a) Shows a set of trials where the robot started at (-22000,0). (b) Trials where the robot started at (-23000, 0).

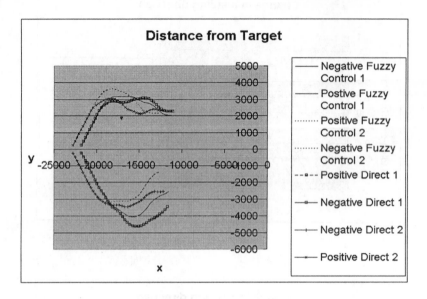

Figure 8.5: The path of the simulated robot with respect to the target object. The legend is the same as for the heading direction graphs Figure 8.4. 1 shows trial set 1 where the robot started at (-22000,0) while 2 shows the second trial set beginning at (-23000,0).

	raw values	fuzzy control
mean	0.0018	0.001
max	0.006	0.003

Figure 8.6: The reduction in the amount of acceleration of the robot. This shows the maximum and the mean change in the robot path given no fuzzy control system, the fuzzy control system applied to the same images as the raw valued trials, and finally the closed loop fuzzy control based trials.

Chapter 9

System Results and Case Studies

This chapter presents the experimental results, which consist of two parts. Firstly, the major components, the recognition and pose determination, are evaluated. [1] The second part of this chapter presents a number of case studies showing the performance of the integrated robot circumnavigation system. The case studies demonstrate the abilities of the whole system to perform the tasks that have been described, and demonstrate the efficacy of the system components that are the subject of this book. The case studies include:

1. moving around the corner of an object;

2. distinguishing a particular object among similar objects;

3. docking;

4. object circumnavigation; and,

5. obstacle avoidance.

9.1 Evaluation of Components

This section presents the evaluation of the vision components of the system which are one of the main contributions of this book. Specifically,

---

[1]Knowledge-based shape-from-shading was evaluated in Chapter 6.

these are: the edge extraction segmentation and matching methods; canonical-views; and, the orientation and position estimators. These are evaluated in isolation from odometry in order to demonstrate their efficacy. In this evaluation, two separate objects were used; a power supply and a model vehicle.

9.1.1 Experimental setup

To evaluate the system, images were taken from a fixed distance from the object, which was rotated on a turntable while the robot and camera remained still. The distances reported are the total distance from the centre of the robot to the centre of the object. The lighting conditions were typical for the Computer Vision and Machine Intelligence Laboratory (CVMIL) at the University of Melbourne. The images within each data set were taken against the same background. However, the background varies between images, and the images from longer distances have a completely different angle due to the space required.

The robot used throughout these experiments was originally a MaxiFander from Denning Branch. It has since been substantially modified to suit the requirements of the laboratory. The robot has a custom-made pan-platform based on a coarse stepper motor. The intervals of the platform are approximately 1°. The camera used is a low cost printed circuit board camera with automatic gain control, mounted in a standard camera housing with an 8.5 mm standard lens. The frame-grabber camera combination is capable of taking 512x512 images. However, 256x256 images are used in this chapter. A second camera is mounted on the side of the robot for obstacle detection, as discussed in Chapter 7 (see Figure 9.1).

Distances stated for the experimental setup have an estimated accuracy of $+/- 50$ mm, and the angles have an estimated accuracy of $+/- 5°$. A set of images was taken initially to set system parameters. Other image sets were then taken for use in these trials.

9.1.2 View matching

A series of images were taken around the power supply at a distance of 1550 mm from 18 angles at intervals of 20° around the object. Five 256x256 images were taken from the same point for each separate angle. The difference between these images is only due to the moment-to-moment variation in lighting and image devices. The background

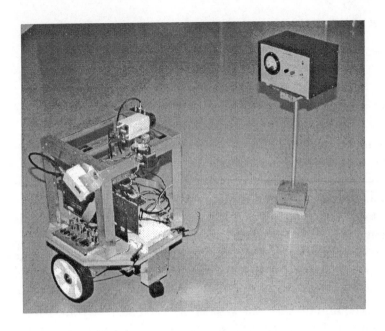

Figure 9.1: The robot navigating around the power supply in the Computer Vision and Machine Intelligence Lab (CVMIL) at the University of Melbourne. The robot is equipped with two cameras, one fixed and pointing forward for obstacle detection, and one on a pan-head for recognising and tracking the object.

to the images is an unmodified section of the laboratory including a filing cabinet, a desk, and power point. Thus, the images include a considerable amount of background clutter. Yellow tape was added along the side and bottom edges of the side surfaces, and along the front surface of the power supply, as there were no features in these places (see Figure 9.3).

There are two separate cases for view matching. Firstly, the *drop-off* problem, where the robot has no *a priori* knowledge of its position. Thus, matching must be performed entirely on the basis of spatial constraints and geometric verification. Also, the *update* case, where the relative position and orientation of the robot is known. A view match was considered to be a *correct* match if the mean distance from the true corner for the predicted corner points was less than 14 pixels. The mean pixel error is defined:

$$error = \sum_{i}^{n} \frac{\sqrt{\Delta x_i^2 + \Delta y_i^2}}{n}, \tag{9.1}$$

where n is the number of points, and Δx and Δy are the differences between the true and expected points in pixels.

A mean pixel error of 14 pixels would occur if all correspondence points were 10 pixels error in both x and y. Note that because real images are used, the true corner is not clear (see Figure 9.2). A sample of a good match is shown in Figure 9.3 (a). A poor match that was still acceptable under this criteria is shown in Figure 9.3 (b). The mismatch of Figure 9.3 (b) is due to the system matching to the outer edge of the double boundary around the object, rather than the inner boundary as modelled. The effect of such mismatches on pose estimation is discussed below.

For the update case, the system matched correctly 90% of the time. Only one of the mismatches was caused by a genuine error in matching when a section of background was matched accidently (see Figure 9.3(c)). This mismatch occurred only for one of the five images taken at the same position. The cause of most of the other mismatches for this data set was matches made to the wrong surface. At the angles where the mismatches occurred, there were two surfaces clearly visible which were approximately the same size. The effects of both types of mismatch on pose estimation are discussed below. A typical example of a match to an incorrect surface is shown in Figure 9.3 (d).

The graph in Figure 9.4 shows the mean pixel distance for all the images. The complete mismatch is at 280°. The error is relatively small as some of the corners were matched correctly. The accepted matches are tightly clustered in around the bottom of the graph.

9.1.3   Pose determination - power supply

This section presents the results of pose determination from image matches. An error analysis of the pose determination technique is presented in Chapter 4. The images are the same set used in the last section view matching. Here pose determination is analysed as part of the system, based on matches to images, with the correspondence errors associated with these matches.

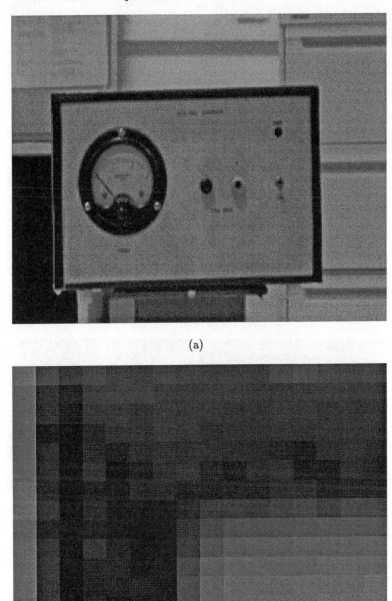

(a)

(b)

Figure 9.2: The precise location of edges is open to interpretation in these images: (a) an image of the front of the power supply object; and, (b) a close up of the upper left-hand corner.

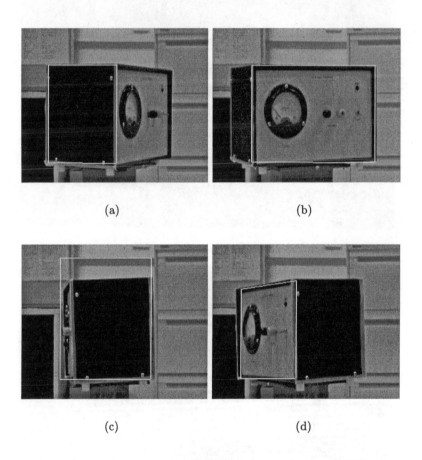

(a)   (b)

(c)   (d)

Figure 9.3: (a) A good match to the correct surface of the power supply. (b) A bad match to the correct surface. Matching has found the outer edge rather than the inner edge. (c) A incorrect match. (d) A match to the wrong surface of the object as a match to the black surface was expected.

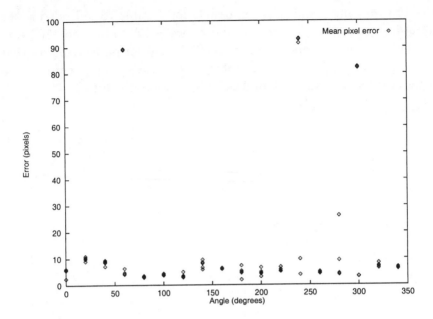

Figure 9.4: The mean pixel error for each match of the set of 90 matches.

Update problem

Two main parameters are estimated: the distance to the object; and the orientation of the object. The distance is the key parameter for motion planning and gaze control. Both the distance to the object and the orientation were considered in the matching process. The estimate of the displacement perpendicular to the image axis has some importance for gaze control. However, the error in the estimate used is large and the actual displacement can only be small relative to the distance to the object if the object is within the image.

For the update problem, Figure 9.5 shows a scatter plot of the distances predicted by the pose determination against the angle from which the image was taken. The actual distance was 1550 *mm*. Figure 9.6 shows a scatter plot of the angle estimates produced. The interpretation of these results is not entirely straightforward in the update case as matching is partly based on estimated distance and orientation. Matches with distance error from the estimate of greater than 15 *mm* were penalised, and values with a distance error of greater than 35 *mm* were discarded. Thus, it is unlikely that a value will fall far outside the 15 *mm* range, and it is impossible for a value to fall outside the 35 *mm* range. Thus, random values between 1400 *mm* and 1700 *mm* would indicate poor pose estimation. Similarly, for pose estimates that differ from the estimate by more than 0.18 radians were penalised, and values differing by more than 0.64 radians were discarded.

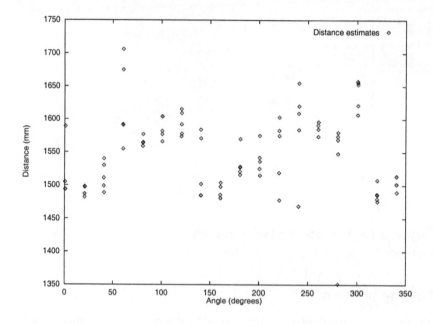

Figure 9.5: Scatter plot of the distances predicted by pose determination against the angle from which the image was taken.

The scatter plot of distance shows that 63% of estimates fell within 50 *mm* of the true value. Only 7% of the estimates fell outside 100 *mm*, all of which correspond to mismatches. Although the matching error was high for these matches, the actual error in pose estimation was small. Thus, an isolated error may not cause the robot to lose the object. The surfaces on this object all have the same height, so a match to the wrong surface will not cause a large error in distance.

All the power supply's surfaces have a similar model, a rectangle. In these trials, no unique marking is modelled for any surface. The front and rear surfaces could be distinguished from the sides when they were nearly parallel to the image plane as they are significantly wider. When either the front or rear surfaces are at a significant angle to the camera the width of the edges will fall within the possible range for the side

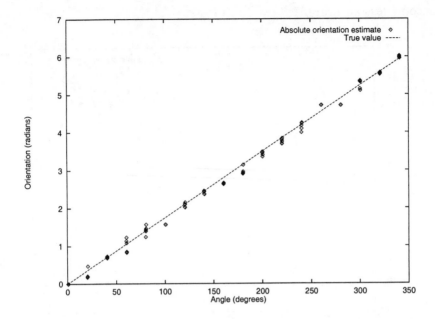

Figure 9.6: Scatter plot of the angle predicted by pose determination against the angle from which the image was taken.

surfaces. From these two graphs it is clear that the mismatches were accepted because they produced distance and pose estimates that were close to what was expected. The largest error in the distance estimate was from the complete mismatch, resulting in an error of 20 mm. The orientation estimate shows a more random scatter within the allowable range (see Figure 9.4).

Varying distances

Images were taken of the power supply at distances of 1850 mm and 2150 mm from robot-to-object to demonstrate that the measures used are stable with respect to distance. Figure 9.7 shows the distance scatter plot for a total of 90 images taken at a distance of 1850 mm, with five images taken at each angle with 20° intervals. Figure 9.8 shows the distance scatter plot for 90 images taken at a distance of 2150 mm with the same angles. It can be seen that the matching is stable at 1850 mm, but starts to degrade at 2150 mm. As the edges become small in the image, the pose determination can be expected to become less accurate.

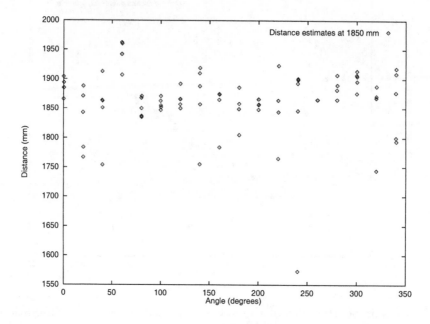

Figure 9.7: Scatter plot of the distance predicted by pose determination against the angle from which the image was taken at a distance of 1850 *mm*.

Drop-off problem

For the drop-off problem, the robot was given information about which of the four views it was facing. However, no information was given about the distance to the object, or the orientation within that view. For this particular object, the model has no features that clearly distinguish between the front and rear surfaces, and between the surfaces of the two sides. It will accept whichever of these appears first in the model. Thus, knowledge of the view was given. Figures 9.9 show the distance predicted for the drop-off problem. It shows that the system was able to match successfully 46% of the time. In most cases, the mismatches were scattered in terms of their prediction of object distance while the correct matches were tightly clustered. This data implies that a naive approach to the drop-off problem will only succeed in 46% of cases, and for some views, may not work at all. However, a more sophisticated start-up procedure requiring multiple consistent matches

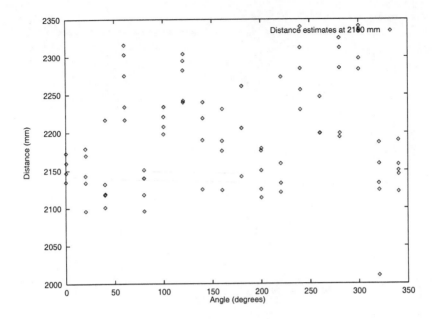

Figure 9.8: Scatter plot of the distance predicted by pose determination against the angle from which the image was taken at a distance of 2150 *mm*.

before any large moves were made may overcome many of these problems. The probability of multiple incorrect matches with a large error in distance estimation is low. It is clear that further consideration of the drop-off problem is necessary.

Incorrect prior position and orientation estimates

In this section, the system is analysed when an incorrect estimate of the distance to the object or orientation of the object is given. To enable comparison, the same data set was used as in previous sections, with the true distance being 1550 *mm*. Six trials were performed with the starting estimate given to be: 1400, 1450, 1500, 1600, 1650, and 1700 *mm*. The distance plots for these estimates are shown in Figures 9.10, 9.11, 9.12, 9.13, 9.14, and 9.15. Two trials are shown with orientation estimates at 0.15 radians above and below the true value. These are shown in Figures 9.16 and 9.17 respectively. Missing points from these graphs are due to matches that the system rejected.

It can be seen that the estimate of the distance to the object was

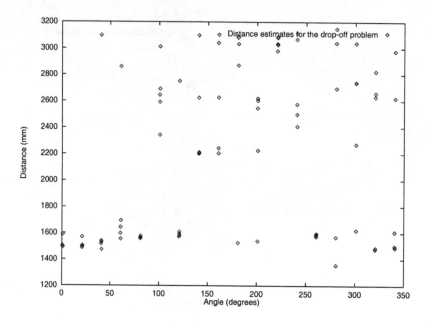

Figure 9.9: Scatter plot of the distance predicted by pose determination against the angle from which the image was taken for the drop-off problem.

quite stable given slightly erroneous *a priori* estimates. There were some small changes in estimates as matches that were accepted with the correct distance estimate that were slightly high or low were penalised for being greater than 150mm from the prior estimate, and so were rejected. This data demonstrates that slight errors in the estimates of the distance to the object will not generally cause the system to diverge.

Matching under partial occlusion

Partial occlusion can occur due to specular reflection, or to obstacles between the robot and the object. A trial was included here to demonstrate that matching is not sensitive to partial occlusion. Figure 9.18 (a) shows the match overlayed on an image when the bottom edge of the object is a almost half occluded. The edges extracted from this image are shown in Figure 9.18 (b). The system was unable to match with the greater amount of occlusion shown in Figure 9.18 (c). The oc-

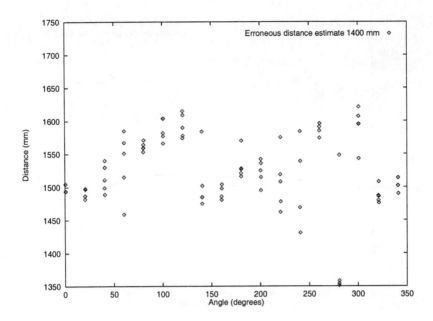

Figure 9.10: Scatter plot of the distance predicted by pose determination against the angle from which the image was taken when the prior estimate of pose was 1400mm (true value was 1550mm). Note that one point at (240,1328), and one at (280,1349) were cut-off by the ranges, in order to keep the format consistent for easy comparison with earlier graphs.

cluding object has a jagged edge to prevent it from generating matches that may lead to false matches. This trail shows that recognition can still occur when a significant proportion of an edge is occluded.

Simulated odometry

A form of simulated odometry was used in order to evaluate the vision system in isolation from odometry errors. Real images and objects were used, but instead of the robot actually moving under its own control, the object was moved manually. However, the errors in object pose estimation were added to the true position for the next image. To allow consistent analysis, the images were the same set used to evaluate view matching and pose determination.

The robot always started at angle 0. It had an estimate of which

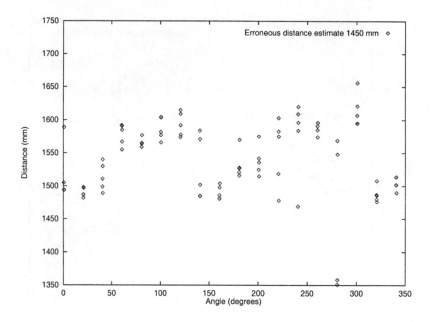

Figure 9.11: Scatter plot of the distance predicted by pose determination against the angle from which the image was taken when the prior estimate of pose was 1450mm (true value was 1550mm). Note that one point at (280,1349) was cut-off by the ranges, in order to keep the format consistent for easy comparison with earlier graphs.

view it was facing, but no estimate of the distance to the object, or its pose. One of the five images for the angle was selected at random. From this image the robot produced a distance, orientation, and displacement estimate. If the system rejected a match, another image was chosen at random from the same set for the current angle, and processed with the same inputs (previously selected images could be selected again). This simulates the case where a match fails, and so the robot takes another image from the same location. Up to five randomly selected images were allowed to be processed before the circumnavigation trial was declared to have failed. The distance and displacement estimates were stored, and 20° was added to the orientation estimate. These new values were used as the position estimate for a randomly selected image from the next angle, 20° further around the object. The estimate found here was also fed forward. The trial terminated when the image from the last set was processed. Thus, each trial consisted of a series of 18

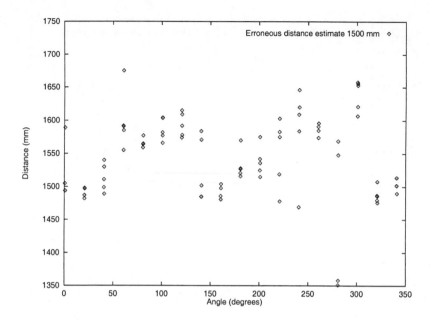

Figure 9.12: Scatter plot of the distance predicted by pose determination against the angle from which the image was taken when the prior estimate of pose was 1500mm (true value was 1550mm). Note that one point at (280,1349) was cut-off by the ranges, in order to keep the format consistent for easy comparison with earlier graphs.

images. 100 trials were performed in this way.

The results from the trials showed the stability of the vision system in isolation. Every trial was a success. The system never diverged away from the object, although for some individual images the match found was wrong. There were only two trials where the system declared an individual match to be a failure and selected another image. In both cases the second image was successful. A composite graph of the distances for the first nine trials is shown in Figure 9.19. It can clearly be seen from this graph that along the paths some large errors in estimation have occurred. However, the system has recovered to have an estimate that is less than 100 *mm* wrong by the last frame in all the cases shown here. The low value at 280° for several runs can be seen to correspond to the incorrect match at 280° in Figure 9.5, and similarly, for the error that occurs in one trial at 60°. Although these were errors in matching, the combined system is able to recover.

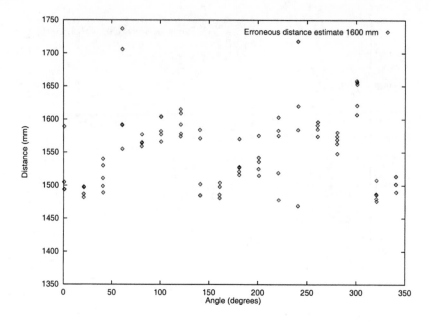

Figure 9.13: Scatter plot of the distance predicted by pose determination against the angle from which the image was taken when the prior estimate of pose was 1600mm (true value was 1550mm).

The data shown for these nine trials is a good representation of all 100 trials.

This trial demonstrates that the system can successfully navigate around this object, assuming that no odometric errors occur, and that the object remains in the frame of the camera.

9.1.4   Pose determination - model vehicle

Matching and pose determination experiments were also carried out with the model vehicle which is shown in Figure 9.20. Matching with this object demonstrates the difficulty of object recognition for guiding mobile robots. The contrast along the edges of the window of the object is sufficient to reliably generate edges, however, these lines are not perfectly straight due to imperfections in the paint-work. On the rear surface, the windscreen wiper always occludes part of the bottom edge of the window, thus a complete edge was never found here. Also, all the views consist of windows in the same position and at the same

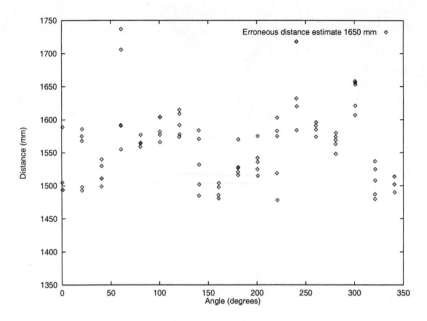

Figure 9.14: Scatter plot of the distance predicted by pose determination against the angle from which the image was taken when the prior estimate of pose was 1650mm (true value was 1550mm).

height. These are divided by many edges of windows which are all close to parallel, and sometimes are only a small distance apart. Further, just above and below each window are edges caused by other features of the car. Finally the windows all have rounded corners. All of these problems make matching difficult with straight-edge matching for this object. The match results for this object were encouraging given these difficulties.

A series of images were taken at 20 degree intervals of the model vehicle, with five images at each angle. Figure 9.21 shows the mean pixel error for each match (mismatches that the system rejected are not included). It can be seen that almost all the matches are acceptable under the previous criteria. Figure 9.22 shows a graph of distance determination plotted against the angle at which the image was taken for the update case. It is clear that the spread of estimated distances is far greater than for the power supply, and is little better than random. Many incorrect matches were rejected by the system. Due to the short vertical length of the edges, a minimal error in the determination of the

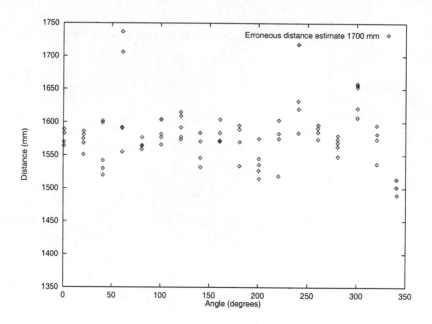

Figure 9.15: Scatter plot of the distance predicted by pose determination against the angle from which the image was taken when the prior estimate of pose was 1700mm (true value was 1550mm).

corner points will lead to a large error in the orientation and distance estimates, relative to the power supply. Such errors can occur easily with this object for the reasons discussed above.

By contrast, the performance for the drop-off problem for this object was significantly better than for the power supply (see Figure 9.23). In this trial, the system was given an estimate only of which view was being faced. In this case, the performance was better than for the update case also. The main features for the power supply were vertical and horizontal edges. These are relatively common in this environment. However, the edges with a vertical component for the model vehicle were all at angles that were uncommon. This is typical of indoor office environments. Thus, mismatches are far less common, and so the drop-off problem is handled relatively well. Based on this evidence, it appears that the rejection criteria based on pose and distance errors were set a too strictly for this object.

For this object, unique determination of which surfaces are currently in view was possible. For a set of four images, one taken from

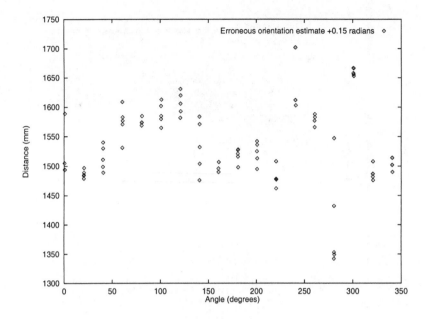

Figure 9.16: Scatter plot of the distance predicted by pose determination against the angle from which the image was taken when the prior estimate of pose was 0.15 radians above the true value.

each side of the object, the correct surface was ranked highest in two cases and second highest for the other two.

9.2 Case Studies

This section presents case studies of the performance of the system as a whole. Specifically, moving around the corners of an object, docking, object circumnavigation, distinguishing a particular object among similar objects, and obstacle avoidance.

9.2.1 Moving around the corner of an object

In this first case study, the robot moves around the corner of the model vehicle. Initially, the robot recognises the object surface of the model vehicle that is clearly visible. The robot moves based on this recognition and then identifies the next view as it becomes visible, while the current view disappears. Tracking-based systems are unable to

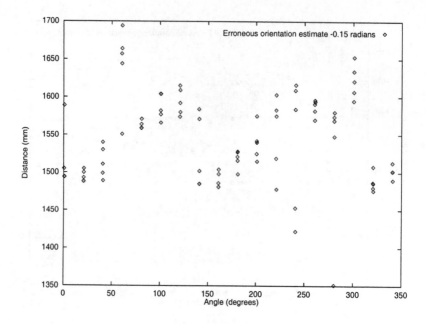

Figure 9.17: Scatter plot of the distance predicted by pose determination against the angle from which the image was taken when the prior estimate of pose was 0.15 radians below the true value.

handle moving around corners in this manner. Moving around corners presents a difficult problem for tracking-based systems, as without a model, what is object and what is background is not well-defined.

In these trials, the system was run in debugging mode, processing a single frame at a time. This was to make the system dump the images that are shown. However, the robot moved based entirely on the control of the system. The system did perform gaze control during these trials. However, part of the object fell slightly outside the camera field of view several times during this set of trials. The camera direction was corrected manually in these cases. Gaze control is discussed in more detail in the circumnavigation experiment below.

Trials with the robot moving around all four corners of the model vehicle are illustrated in Figures 9.24, 9.25, 9.26, and 9.27. These figures show the images taken by the robot for recognition, while the overlayed lines show the part recognised. The front and rear windows make up the model for the front and rear of the car. The rear and middle windows are modelled for the side surfaces. The figures only

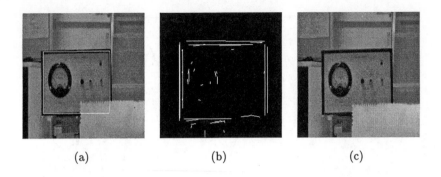

(a)   (b)   (c)

Figure 9.18: The matching method is tolerant of some occlusion. (a) The robot matches this image where almost half of the bottom edge is occluded. (b) The edges extracted on which the match was based. (c) The robot was unable to match this image with slightly greater occlusion.

show the match to the left-most of the windows for the side surfaces. It can be seen that the robot has misrecognised the surfaces in Figure 9.24 (b) and (c), Figure 9.25 (b), and Figure 9.27 (b) and (c). However, the robot recovers in subsequent frames.

In Figure 9.24, the robot has matched the model for the rear window to the middle window in (b). As a consequence of this mismatch, the robot looks for the view of the front window earlier than it should, and so in (c) matches the model for the front window to the side windows. The system then recovers in (d). In Figure 9.25 (b), the robot has matched to the wrong part of the object. However, it recovers in (c) to match to the side surfaces.

In Figure 9.27 (b), the robot has matched the model for the middle window to the front side window, while the model for the rear window is matched to the middle window. In (c), the robot has mismatched the model for the middle window to the panel between the front and middle windows. At first impression, it might be considered that this would lead to a poor estimation of the object pose, however, the pose estimation is based on the four most distant points in the match. As the match to the rear window (not shown in this image) is reasonable, the final pose estimate is accurate. Thus, the system is able to recover in (d). However, it would be preferable if such matches were rejected.

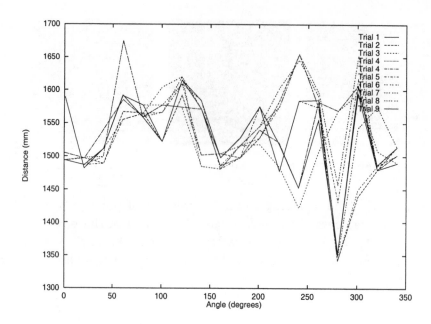

Figure 9.19: The distance plots for the first nine trials of simulated circumnavigation.

9.2.2 Distinguishing a particular object among similar objects

Figure 9.28(a) shows an image in which two cars are present, with one in front of the other. The robot can uniquely identify either car depending on which model it is given. In Figure 9.28(a) it identifies the front car, and in (b) the rear car from the same image. The object model is read in from a file. An extract from a model file is shown in Appendix 3.

9.2.3 Docking

This section demonstrates an application of circumnavigation to the docking problem. The robot is expected to recognise the object, and move around it until the required surface is found, and then move in close to that surface. Figure 9.29 shows a graph of the movement of the robot around the power supply object. The robot is initially at the front surface of the object. Due to the ambiguity of this object, as discussed in the previous section, the system is given knowledge of

Figure 9.20: The model vehicle used in these experiments.

the surface it is facing when it starts. The robot moves around to the surface to the right of the front surface. As soon as this surface is recognised, the system moves to dock with it. Figure 9.30 shows the images that the robot took as it moved, as well as the matches that were made. Figure 9.30 (b) shows the only significant mismatch for this trial which occurred due to a bug in the implementation of the edge segmentation module. The right-hand side edge of the power supply has been slightly mislocated.

The experiment shown in Figures 9.31 and 9.32 was performed by an early prototype of the robot system, before the robot motion control system was fully developed. Hence, the experiment demonstrates view planning rather than navigation as the robot was moved manually between each view designated by the system. This experiment is included to demonstrate another example of docking, and the quadratic matching for curved edges. The front windscreen of the model car in this experiment has curved edges, thus, in order to recognise it, the quadratic edge extrapolation method was required for edge segmentation. The experiment shows how the system could perform in an industrial setting. The robot identifies the car, moves around it in a

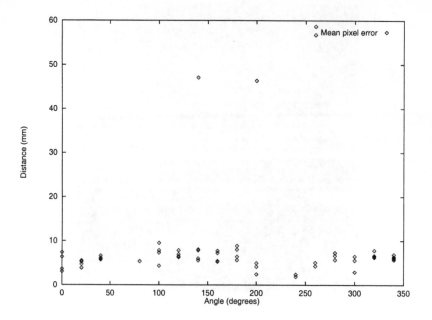

Figure 9.21: Scatter plot of the mean pixel errors for the matches to the model vehicle against the angle from which the image was taken at a distance of 1400mm when the position of the object was available.

clockwise direction, and then moves close to the rear right-hand corner for docking.

The quadratic matching method relied on extracting almost the entire edge. The method was found to be sensitive to specular reflections, and so is not reliable in practice without further development.

9.2.4   Object circumnavigation

In this case study, the robot demonstrates circumnavigation of the power supply, where the system guides the robot around the object, and finally returns to its starting position. Figure 9.33 shows a graph of the robot moving around the object. This graph is to scale, and was constructed by marking the robot positions as it moved, then measuring them manually after the experiment was completed. The positions shown are accurate to within 100 *mm*. Figure 9.34 and 9.35 show the images from which the robot recognised the object. These are overlayed with the matches that were made. The robot clearly mismatches the

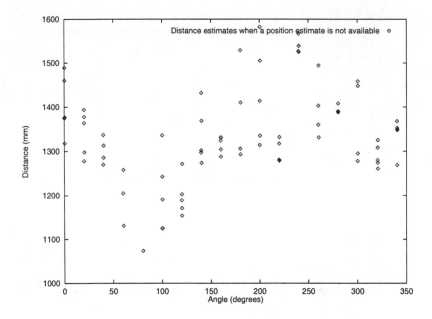

Figure 9.22: Scatter plot of the distance predicted by pose determination for the model vehicle against the angle from which the image was taken at a distance of 1400mm. Here an estimate of object position was available.

object in the frames (e), (g), (i), and (n), with some slight mismatches in other frames. However, these mismatches were not sufficient for the robot to lose the object. The robot did not lose the object quickly as matching discards matches that lead to pose estimates that are far from the previous pose estimate.

The data shown are part of a longer run of 39 images, where the robot moved around the object $1\frac{3}{4}$ times, before being unable to match the object. During this run, the object fell narrowly outside the field of view of the camera after the image of Figure 9.34 (a), (g), (i), and (k), and Figure 9.35 (b), (f), and (h). In all, during the 39 movements around the object, the camera moved so that object was lost on 13 occasions, i.e., one third of the time. Many of these faults corresponded to mismatches. However, gaze control was not an initial aim of this book, and is a difficult problem in its own right. Thus, performance of this standard was considered more than satisfactory.

Five trials of circumnavigation were conducted in order to assess

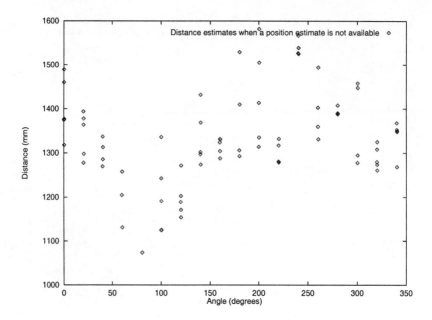

Figure 9.23: Scatter plot of the distance predicted by pose determination for the model vehicle against the angle from which the image was taken at a distance of 1400mm. Here an estimate of object position was not available.

the reliability of the system. A trial was considered to succeed if the robot progressed around the object to return to its initial position. A trial failed if the robot failed to match the object five times in a row, or if the robot accepted three incorrect matches in a row. These are detected failure, and undetected failure cases respectively. For the five trials, two were successful, one resulted in a detected failure, and two resulted in undetected failures.

The system is not reliable as it stands. Further, failures should be detected promptly. However, this performance is not unexpected because issues of uncertainty and robustness were considered outside the scope of this book.

9.2.5   Obstacle avoidance

Although obstacle avoidance is not a core function of the system, it has been included here to demonstrate that the knowledge-based approach enables effective handling of additional environmental complex-

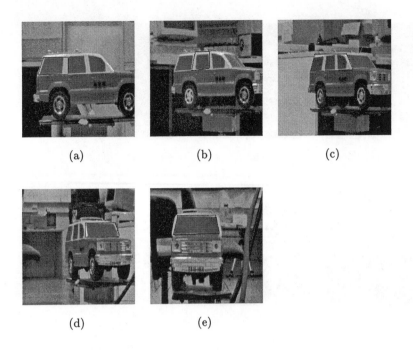

Figure 9.24: Moving around the first corner of the object.

ities. The system does not rely on a complete *a priori* knowledge of the environment. Obstacle avoidance is performed reactively, and so allows some potential for change in the environment. In this, the robot uses a simple obstacle avoidance strategy, as shown in Figure 9.36. On detecting an obstacle, the robot backs off and proceeds to the destination surface in the other direction.

This experiment was performed with an earlier version of the system, which used a different edge matching technique, and for which the odometry subsystem was not fully integrated. The odometry subsystem was reset between moves. However, the path planning is still identical to the current system, and so still forms a meaningful demonstration.

9.3 Conclusion

These experiments demonstrate that the robot system is able to uniquely identify an object and move around it, while maintaining knowledge of the object's relative position. The system is able to handle different

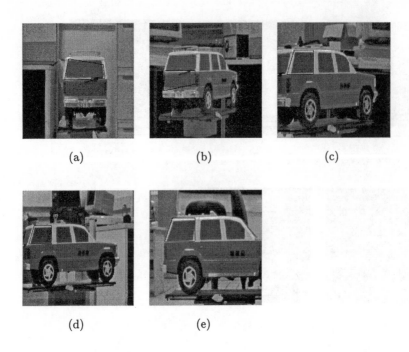

Figure 9.25: Moving around the second corner of the object.

objects as specified in the model. This chapter also demonstrated the system performing circumnavigation and docking.

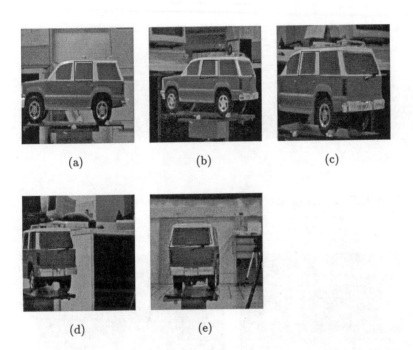

(a)   (b)   (c)

(d)   (e)

Figure 9.26: Moving around the third corner of the object.

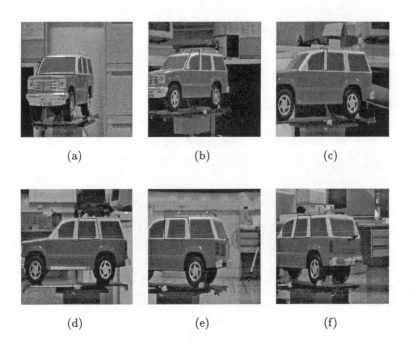

Figure 9.27: Moving around the fourth corner of the object.

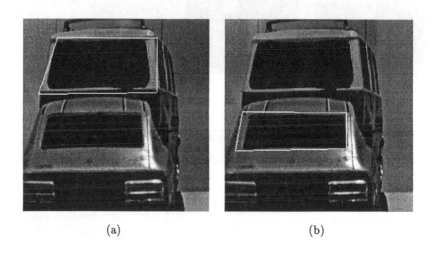

Figure 9.28: The robot can uniquely identify either car depending on which model is specified.

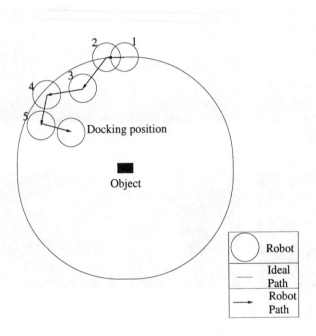

Figure 9.29: Docking with the power supply. This diagram is to scale.

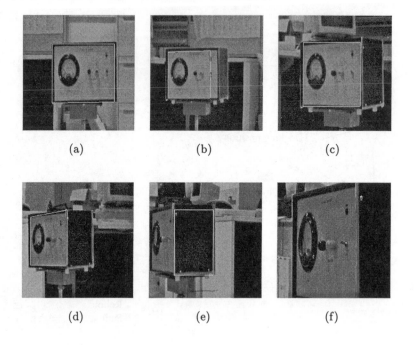

Figure 9.30: Docking with the power supply: (a) - (d) the robot recognises the power supply and moves accordingly; (e) the robot recognises the required surface, and then moves in to dock; and, (f) the robot moves in to dock.

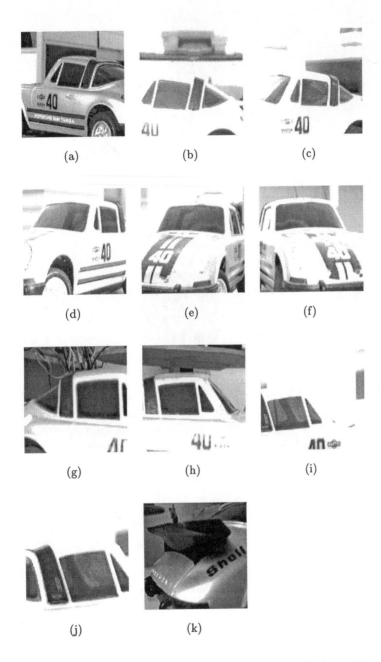

Figure 9.31: Camera images of car from experimental run: (a) initial view, (b) to (j) views chosen by the robot, (k) docking view (rear right-hand corner of the car).

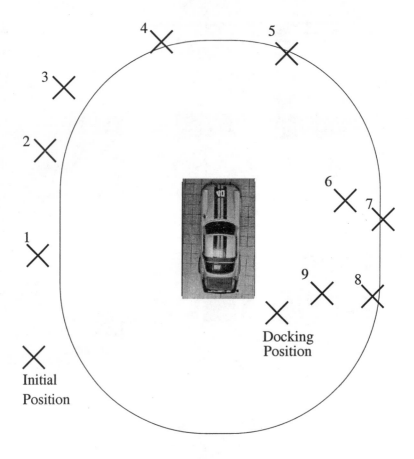

Figure 9.32: Expected positions versus the ideal path (the solid line) around the object. The actual docking position is the rear right hand corner of the car.

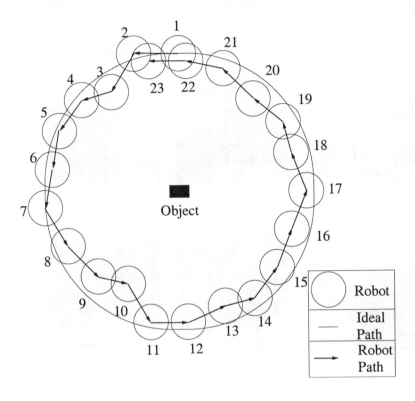

Figure 9.33: Circumnavigating the power supply. This diagram is to scale, measurements are to the nearest 100 mm.

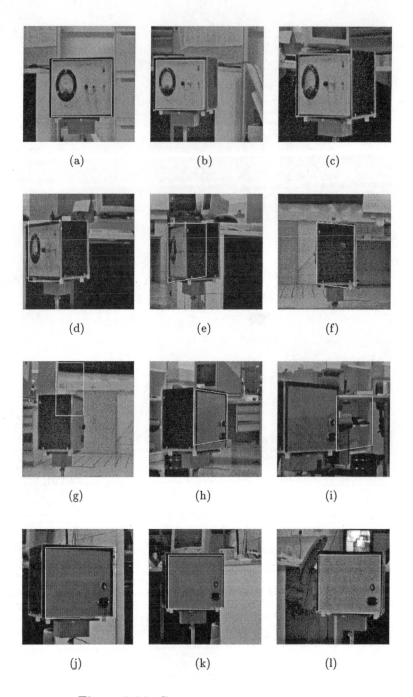

Figure 9.34: Circumnavigating the power supply.

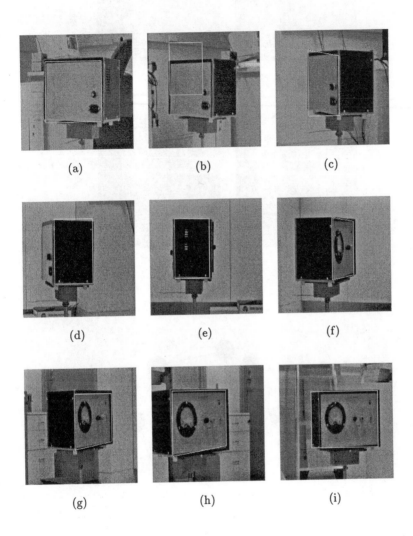

Figure 9.35: Circumnavigating the power supply. (cont.)

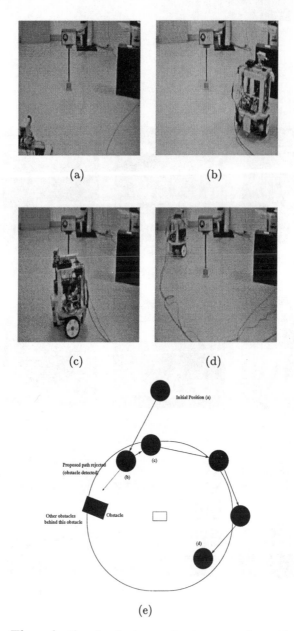

Figure 9.36: The robot's aim is to navigate around to the back surface of the power supply, while an obstacle blocks its path. (a) The starting position. (b) The robot detects that the obstacle (SGI workstation, the dark box in the image) is blocking its path for travelling counter-clockwise around the object. (c) The robot turns around and begins travelling clockwise around the object. (d) The robot at the final destination. (e) Schematic of the path taken.

Chapter 10

Conclusion

This book has presented a vision system for guiding a robot around a known object. The approach taken differs from previous vision-guided mobile robot systems detailed in the literature and suggests a new direction in research in this field. This vision system found its position in relation to a single known object, rather than localising based on simple features extracted from many items in the environment. In order to navigate based on information from a single object, more complex features must be derived from the object to give reasonable certainty of correct identification. As such, the approach applied novel high-level vision techniques that took account of relative edge position using geometric verification based on a model. The book also presented a method for integrating shape determination.

A framework of conceptual embodiment was proposed, in order to apply high-level vision to robot navigation. A novel method for recognising objects was developed using conceptual embodiment, along with a method for knowledge-based shape-from-shading. The methods developed based on conceptual embodiment were efficacious for guiding mobile robot navigation, as demonstrated theoretically and through experimental results.

To facilitate object recognition, this book introduced canonical-views. This is the first object representation that has been specifically designed for mobile robot navigation. The canonical-view representation supported reliable object recognition from a large range of possible robot locations relative to the object for the scenarios presented.

A novel method for edge segmentation was also developed for use with canonical-views. This method was designed for fast processing to suit the requirements of robot navigation. Fast processing was achieved by performing the majority of image analysis at a coarse scale, as well as operating on windows rather than pixels. Also, roughly clustering edge segments based on orientation and position in the image reduced the computation required for connected components analysis.

A mobile robot system must not require human intervention, so a new method was needed for shape-from-shading. A knowledge-based approach was taken in order to automate shape-from-shading, and to handle manufactured objects. This book presented a knowledge-based approach to the shape-from-shading problem. As well, a new approach was derived in order to find a unique solution along an orientation discontinuity when a partial object model is available. This method was able to recover shape in images for which existing systems would be unable to find a unique solution. Further, the method converges faster than comparable algorithms by applying domain knowledge.

Canonical-views and the edge matching technique were integrated with existing methods for robot navigation into a complete robot navigation system. Extensive trials demonstrate that the methods produced are efficacious for robot navigation. The system demonstrated:

- navigating around corners;

- unique identification;

- docking;

- circumnavigation; and,

- obstacle avoidance.

The results demonstrated that the techniques of high-level vision can be applied usefully to guide a mobile robot.

This book also presented a fuzzy control system for application to fixation-based vision-guided docking. This demonstrated that fuzzy control can be used effectively for vision-guided mobile robot navigation.

10.1 Limitations of the Research Presented and Future Work

This is an ambitious research project aimed to incorporate many disparate threads of research into a single system for robot navigation.

The research presented is the first attempt at the circumnavigation problem, and as such, sets a standard for future systems in this area. Many of the individual components have limitations that can be improved upon. These improvements, and issues of robustness and uncertainty were beyond the scope of this book. Some further developments that would improve the system include:

- The primary goal of the research is to build computer vision systems for robot navigation, rather than construct the navigation methods themselves. Hence, the methods used for navigation can be improved. The navigation system generated discrete path segments for the robot to follow, which lead to the robot performing stops and turns as it moves. Stopping and starting are causes of wheel-slippage and hence, frequent stopping and starting leads to large errors in odometry. By using a potential field-based approach, smoother trajectories can be achieved, which may lead to a reduction in odometric errors.

- Although in this book a knowledge-based approach for supporting edge matching with additional information has been developed, this method was not integrated with the edge matching for use in navigation trials. In the matching results presented, there were several occasions where slight mismatches could have been corrected by knowledge-based analysis. For example, Figure 9.3 (b) shows an image where the system was intended to match the edges of a window, but instead matched an edge on a neighbouring window. Such mismatches could be corrected if some analysis of the region within the match were performed. By using the knowledge-based architecture presented in Chapter 5, the colour of the region internal to the match could be analysed at a coarse scale. In the present matching system, there is no mechanism for appropriately penalising this type of mismatch as the geometric error for this match is small.

- The system performed gaze control based on the estimated object position in odometric coordinates. This method was adequate when matches to the object were correct and pose estimation was accurate. However, this gaze control method is not sufficiently robust for long paths around the object with erroneous matches. The system did not make use of continuity of edge positions between images. When the robot progresses around a corner and current edges become occluded, edge positions clearly will not be continuous. However, if the image sampling is frequent, then the movements of edges between images would be small, and the current edge position could be fed back into edge extraction for the next image. Thus, edge extraction could be performed within an image region, as well as within an orientation. This may make mismatches of image edges less likely when given an initial correct match. Such processing would also require a smaller portion of the image to have edge extraction performed, and reduce the number of match candidates. With such an approach, gaze control could be performed directly in image coordinates rather than in odometric coordinates. Also, any divergence between gaze direction predictions based on image and odometric coordinates could provide an early warning of matching problems.

- The edge segmentation method presented was developed to support the current requirements of the system. The principal of segmentation at a coarse scale, with final processing at a pixel scale could be extended to a full multi-scale technique. It would remain an empirical question as to whether such a general multi-scale technique would outperform existing methods for finding straight edges.

- The use of fuzzy control was only trialled in simulation for a restricted application. Fuzzy control could also assist with gaze control and smoothing the robot's path.

- Finally, an automated mechanism for constructing canonical-views would be a major step forward for the system. Many values could be taken directly from geometric specifications for a manufactured object. However, the relative spatial features, and the correspondence points that are used for pose estimation could also be automatically derived from CAD models. Automatically selecting model features based on images of the object under the required conditions would be a challenging task.

The system presented in this book is a step toward the vision of a new generation of autonomous robots. The book has demonstrated that high-level vision techniques can be successfully applied to autonomous robots in order to solve difficult problems such as circumnavigation and docking.

10.2   Extended quotation from Descartes

> . . . *if there were machines which bore a resemblance to*
> *our body and imitated our actions as far as it was morally*
> *possible to do so, we should always have two very certain*
> *tests by which to recognise that, for all that, they were not*
> *real men. The first is, that they could never use speech or*
> *signs as we do when placing our thoughts on record for the*
> *benefit of others. For we can easily understand a machine's*
> *being constituted so that it can utter words, even emit some*
> *responses to action on it of a corporeal kind, which brings*
> *about a change in its organs; for instance, if it is touched*
> *in a particular part it may ask what we wish to say to it; if*
> *in another part it may exclaim that it is being hurt, and so*
> *on. But it never happens that it arranges its speech in var-*
> *ious ways, in order to reply to appropriately to everything*
> *that may be said in its presence, as even the lowest type*
> *of man can do. And the second difference is, that although*
> *machines can perform certain things as well as or perhaps*
> *better than any of us can do, they infallibly fall short in oth-*
> *ers, by the which means we may discover that they did not*
> *act from knowledge, but only from the disposition of their*
> *organs. For while reason is a universal instrument which*
> *can serve for all contingencies, these organs have need of*
> *some special adaptation for every particular action. From*
> *this follows that it is morally impossible that there should*
> *be sufficient diversity in any machine to allow it to act in*
> *all the events of life in the same way as our reason causes*
> *us to act.*

R. Descarte. circa 1628. [95]

Bibliography

[1] *The Macquarie Dictionary*. Macquarie library: Macquarie University, AUSTRALIA, 1989.

[2] Y Aloimonos. *Active Perception*. Lawrance Erlbaum Assoc., Hillsdale, NJ, 1993.

[3] Y Aloimonos. Introduction: Active vision revisited. In *Active Perception*, pages 1–18. Lawrance Erlbaum Assoc., Hillsdale, NJ, 1993.

[4] Y Aloimonos, I Weiss, and A Bandopadhay. Active vision. *International Journal of Computer Vision*, 7:333–356, 1988.

[5] R C Arkin and D MacKenzie. Temporal coordination of perceptual algorithms for mobile robot navigation. *IEEE Trans on Robotics and Automation*, 10(3):276–286, June 1994.

[6] R C Arkin and R R Murphy. Autonomous navigation in a manufacturing environment. *IEEE Trans. on Robotics and Automation*, 6(4):445–454, August 1990.

[7] S Assilian. *Artificial Intelligence in the Control of Real Dynamical Systems*. PhD thesis, London University, 1974.

[8] N Ayache and O D Faugeras. Maintaining representations of the environment of a mobile robot. *IEEE Trans. on Robotics and Automation*, 5(6), Dec. 1989.

[9] N Ayache, O D Faugeras, F Lustman, and Z Zhang. Visual navigation of a mobile robot: Recent steps. In *Robots: Coming of Age. Proceedings of the International Symposium and Exposition on Robots. Designated the 19th ISIR by the International Federation of Robotics.*, pages 725–740, 1988.

[10] D H Ballard. Animate vision. *Artificial Intelligence*, 48(1):57–86, 1991.

[11] N M Barnes and Z Q Liu. Model-based circumnavigating autonomous robots. Technical Report 12, Dept. of Computer Science, Univ. of Melbourne., 1995.

[12] N M Barnes and Z Q Liu. Vision guided circumnavigating autonomous robots. In *ICSC '95 - Proc. Third International Computer Science Conference: Image Analysis Applications and Computer Graphics, Hong Kong*, pages 33–42, Dec. 1995.

[13] N M Barnes and G Sandini. Direction control for an active docking behaviour based on the rotational component of log-polar optic flow. In *European Conference on Computer Vision 2000*, volume 2, pages 167–181, 2000.

[14] B Barsham and H F Durrant-Whyte. Inertial navigation systems for mobile robots. *IEEE Trans. on Robotics and Automation*, 11(3):328–342, June 1995.

[15] S S Beauchemin and J L Barron. The computation of optical flow. *ACM Computing Surveys*, 27(3):433–467, 1996.

[16] J Ben-Arie. The probabilistic peaking effect of viewed angles and distances with application to 3-d object recognition. *IEEE Trans. on Pattern Analysis and Machine Intelligence*, 12(8):760–774, 1990.

[17] J Bennet. *Kant's Analytic* Cambridge University Press:Cambridge, England, 1966.

[18] A Bernardino and J Santos-Victor. Binocular tracking: integrating perception and control. *IEEE Trans. on Robotics and Automation*, 15(6), Dec. 1999.

[19] I Biederman. *Perceptual Organisation*, chapter On the Semantics of a Glance at a Scene, pages 213–253. Lawrance Erlbaum Assoc., Hillsdale, NJ, 1981.

[20] I Biederman. Recognition-by-components: A theory of human image understanding. *Psychological Review*, 94(2):115–147, 1987.

[21] J Billingsley and M Schoenfish. Automatic guidance of agricultural vehicles. In *Robots for Australian Industries: Proc. 1995 Nat. Conf. of the Australian Robot Association, Melbourne, 5-7 July*, pages 25–32, 1995.

[22] J Borenstein and Y Koren. The vector field histogram - fast obstacle avoidance for mobile robots. *IEEE Trans. Robotics and Automation*, 7(3):278–288, June 1991.

[23] D J Braunegg. Marvel: A system that recognizes world location with stereo vision. *IEEE Trans. Robotics and Automation*, 9(3):303–308, June 1993.

[24] M J Brooks and B K P Horn. Shape and source from shading. In B K P Horn and M J Brooks, editors, *Shape From Shading*, pages 53–68. The MIT Press: Cambridge Massachusetts, London England, 1989.

[25] R A Brooks. Model-based three-dimensional interpretations of two-dimensional images. *IEEE Trans. on Pattern Analysis and Machine Intelligence*, PAMI-5(2):140–150, March 1983.

[26] R A Brooks. Solving the find-path problem by good representation of free space. *IEEE Trans. on Systems, Man, and Cybernetics*, SMC-13(3), March-April 1983.

[27] R A Brooks. Visual map making for a mobile robot. *IEEE Int. Conf. on Robotics and Automation*, pages 824–829, 1985.

[28] R A Brooks. Achieving artifical intelligence through building robots. Technical Report 899, MIT Artificial Intelligence Laboratory, 1986.

[29] R A Brooks. A robust layered control system for a mobile robot. *IEEE Journal of Robotics and Automation*, RA-2(1):14–23, 1986.

[30] R A Brooks. Intelligence without reason. Technical Report 1293, MIT Artificial Intelligence Laboratory, April 1991.

[31] R A Brooks. Intelligence without representation. *Artificial Intelligence*, 47(1-3):139–160, 1991.

[32] A R Bruss. The eikonal equation: Some results applicable to computer vision. In B K P Horn and M J Brooks, editors, *Shape*

From Shading, pages 69–87. The MIT Press: Cambridge Massachusetts, London England, 1989.

[33] J B Burns and E M Riseman. Matching complex images to multiple 3d objects using view description networks. In *IEEE Computer Society Conf. on Computer Vision and Patt ern Recognition*, pages 328–334, 1992.

[34] J B Burns, R S Weiss, and E M Riseman. View variation of point-set and line-segment features. *IEEE Trans. on Pattern Analysis and Machine Intelligence*, 15(1):51–68, Jan. 1993.

[35] D Burschka and G Farber. Active controlled exploration of 3d environmental models based on a binocular stereo system. In *8th International Conference on Advanced Robotics. Proceedings. ICAR'97*, pages 971–977, 1997.

[36] O I Camps, L G Shapiro, and R M Haralick. Premio: An overview (object recognition). In *Workshop on Directions in Automated CAD-Based Vision*, pages 11–21, 1991.

[37] J Canny and B Donald. Simplified voronoi diagrams. *Discrete Comput. Geom.*, 3(3):219–236, 1988.

[38] J F Canny. Finding edges and lines in images. Master's thesis, MIT Artificial Intelligence Laboratory, Massachusetts Institute of Technology, Massachusetts, 1983.

[39] Karel Capek. *R. U. R. (Rossum's Universal Robots)*. Oxford University Press, London, 1942.

[40] V Chandran and W W Boles. Object recognition using higher-order spectral and wavelet tranform based features. In *Workshop on Robotics and Robot Vision at ISSPA'96: 4th International Symposium on Signal Processing and its Applications*, pages 44–49, Aug. 1996.

[41] S Chen and H Freeman. On the characteristic views of quadric-surfaced solids. In *Proc. IEEE Workshop Directions Automated Cad-Based Vision*, pages 34–43, 1991.

[42] T R Collins, A M Henshaw, R C Arkin, and W D Webster. Narrow aisle mobile robot navigation in hazardous environments.

In *Transactions of the Ameraican Nuclear Society*, volume 70, pages 411–412, June 1994.

[43] I J Cox. Blanche - an experiment in guidance and navigation of an autonomous robot vehicle. *IEEE Trans. on Robotics and Automation*, 7(2):193–204, 1991.

[44] F Cozman and E Krotkov. Automatic mountain detection and pose estimation for teleoperation of lunar rovers. In *IEEE Int. Conf. on Robotics and Automation*, pages 2452–7, April 1997.

[45] J D Crisman and C E Thorpe. SCARF: A color vision system that tracks roads and intersections. *IEEE Trans. on Robotics and Automation*, 9(1), Feb. 1993.

[46] J D Crisman and J A Webb. The warp machine on navlab. *IEEE Trans. on Pattern Analysis and Machine Intelligence*, 13(5):451–465, May 1991.

[47] S Dance and T Caelli. A symbolic object-oriented picture interpretation network: Soopin. In *Proceedings of the International Workshop on Structural and Syntactic Pattern Recognition*, pages 530–541, 1992.

[48] Sandy Dance, Terry Caelli, and Zhi-Qiang Liu. A concurrent, hierarchical approach to symbolic dynamic scene interpretation. *Pattern Recognition Journal*, 29(11):1891–1903, 1996.

[49] E R Davies. *Machine Vision: Theory, Algorithms, Practicalities*. Academic Press, London, 1990.

[50] R Davis. Expert systems: Where are we? and where do we go from here? In O N Garcia and Y-T Chien, editors, *Knowledge-Based Systems: Fundamentals and Tools*, pages 7–26. IEEE Computer Society Press, Los Alamitos, California, 1992.

[51] F Dellaert, D Pomerleau, and C Thorpe. Model-based car tracking integrated with a road-follower. In *Proceedings of the IEEE Int. Conf. on Robotics and Automation*, volume 3, pages 1889–94, May 1998.

[52] S J Dickinson, H I Christensen, J K Tsotsos, and G Olofsson. Active object recognition integrating attention and viewpoint

control. *Computer Vision, Graphics, and Image Understanding*, 67(3):239–260, September 1997.

[53] S J Dickinson and D Metaxas. Integrating qualitative and quantitive shape recovery. *International Journal of Computer Vision*, 13(3):311–330, 1994.

[54] S J Dickinson, A P Pentland, and A Rosenfeld. From volumes to views: An approach to 3-d object recognition. *Computer Vision, Graphics, and Image Processing*, 55(2):130–154, March 1992.

[55] S J Dickinson, S Stevenson, E Amdur, J Tsotsos, and L Olsson. Integrating task-directed planning with reactive object recognition. In *Proceedings SPIE:Intelligent Robots and Computer Vision X11:Algorithms and Techniques*, pages 212–224, 1993.

[56] E D Dickmanns and V Graefe. Applications of dynamic monocular machine vision. *Machine Vision and Applications*, 1(4):241–261, 1988.

[57] E D Dickmanns and V Graefe. Dynamic monocular machine vision. *Machine Vision and Applications*, 1(4):223–240, 1988.

[58] Z Dodds and G D Hager. A color interest operator for landmark-based navigation. In *14th National Conference on Artificial Intelligence.*, pages 655–660, Providence, Rhode Island, 1997.

[59] B Draper, A Hanson, and E Riseman. Knowledge-directed vision: Control, learning and integration. *Proceedings of the IEEE*, 84(11):1625–1637, Nov. 1996.

[60] B A Draper, R T Collins, J Brolio, A R Hanson, and E M Riseman. The schema system. *International Journal of Computer Vision*, 2(3):209–250, 1989.

[61] H L Dreyfus. *What Computers Still Can't Do: A Critique of Artifical Reasoning.* The MIT Press:Cambridge, Mass., 1994.

[62] Y Du and N P Papanikolopoulos. Real-time vehicle following through a novel symmetry-based approach. In *IEEE Int. Conf. on Robotics and Automation*, pages 3160–5, April 1997.

[63] H Dulimarta and A K Jain. Mobile robot localization in indoor environment. *Pattern Recognition Journal*, 30(1):99–111, 1997.

[64] J Dupré. *The disorder of things : metaphysical foundations of the disunity of science.* Harvard University Press, Cambridge, Mass, 1993.

[65] P Dupuis and John Oliensis. An optimal control formulation and related numerical methods for a problem in shape reconstruction. *The Annals of Applied Probability,* 4(2):287–346, 1994.

[66] H F Durrant-Whyte. An autonomous guided vehicle for cargo handling operations. *Journal of Robotics Research,* 15(5):407–440, Oct. 1996.

[67] K Ebihara, T Otani, and E Kume. Position localisation for mobile robots using a colour image of equipment at nuclear plants. *Robotica,* 14(6):677–685, Nov.-Dec. 1993.

[68] Y Edan. Design of an autonomous agricultural robot. *Artificial Intelligence: the international journal of artificial intelligence, neural networks, and complex problem solving technologies.,* 5(1):41–50, 1995.

[69] D Eggert and K Bowyer. Perspective projection aspect graphs of solids of revolution: An implementation. In *Proc. Second Int. Conf. on Computer Vision,* pages 44–53, 1991.

[70] D W Eggert and K W Bowyer. Computing the perspective projection aspect graph of solids of revolution. *IEEE Trans. on Pattern Analysis and Machine Intelligence,* 15(2):109–128, Feb. 1993.

[71] D W Eggert, K W Bowyer, C R Dyer, H I Christensen, and D B Goldof. The scale space aspect graph. *IEEE Trans. on Pattern Analysis and Machine Intelligence,* 15(11):1114–1130, Nov. 1993.

[72] A Elfes. Sonar-based real-world mapping and navigation. *IEEE Journal of Robotics and Automation,* 3(3):249–265, 1987.

[73] A Elfes. Using occupancy grids for mobile robot perception and navigation. *IEEE Computer,* 22(6):46–57, 1989.

[74] J D Erickson, K A Grimm, T W Pendleton, L E Howard, R A Goode, M S Hawkins, D Bloss, J A Seaborn, C S Hess, D Walker, D E Phinney, R S Norsworthy, G Anderson, C H

Chien, L Hewgill, M Littlefield, and F Gaudiano. An intelligent space robot for crew help and crew and equipment retrieval. *Applied Intelligence*, 5(1):7–39, 1995.

[75] H R Everett. *Sensors for mobile robots: theory and application.* A K Peters, Wellesley MA, 1995.

[76] O Faugeras, J Mundy, N Ahuja, C Dyer, A Pentland, R Jain, and K Ikeuchi. Why aspect graphs are not (yet) practical for computer vision. In *Workshop on Directions in Automated CAD-Based Vision*, pages 97–104, 1991.

[77] F P Ferrie and M D Levine. Where and why local shading analysis works. *IEEE Trans. on Pattern Analysis and Machine Intelligence*, 11(2):198–206, Feb. 1989.

[78] R Fikes and T Kehler. The role of frame-based representation in reasoning. *Communications of the ACM*, 28(9):904–920, 1985.

[79] P J Flynn and A K Jain. Bonsai: 3-d object recognition using constrained search. *IEEE Trans. on Pattern Analysis and Machine Intelligence*, 13(10):1066–1075, 1991.

[80] O N Garcia and Y-T Chien. Introduction. In O N Garcia and Y-T Chien, editors, *Knowledge-Based Systems: Fundamentals and Tools*, pages 1–6. IEEE Computer Society Press, Los Alamitos, California, 1992.

[81] W F Gardner and D T Lawton. Interactive model-based vehicle tracking. *IEEE Trans. on Pattern Analysis and Machine Intelligence*, 18(11):1115–1121, Nov. 1996.

[82] G Garibotto, S Masciangelo, M Ilic, and P Bassino. Service robotics in logistic automation: Robolift: Vision based autonomous navigation of a conventional fork-lift for pallet handling. In *8th International Conference on Advanced Robotics. Proceedings. ICAR'97*, pages 781–6, 1997.

[83] E Gat. *Artificial Intelligence and Mobile Robots*, chapter Three-layer architectures. AIII Press/MIT Press, Menlo Park, California, USA, 1998.

[84] E Gat, M G Slack, D P Miller, and R J Firby. Path planning and execution monitoring for a planetary rover. *IEEE Int. Conf. on Robotics and Automation*, pages 20–25, 1990.

[85] M P Georgeff and A L Lansky. Procedural knowledge. *Proceedings of the IEEE*, 74(10):1383–1398, 1986.

[86] Z Gigus and J Malik. Computing the aspect graph for line drawings of polyhedral objects. *IEEE Trans. on Pattern Analysis and Machine Intelligence*, 12(2):113–122, 1990.

[87] S Gil, R Milanese, and T Pun. Feature selection for object tracking in traffic scenes. In *Proceedings SPIE:Intelligent Vehicle Highway Systems*, volume 2344, pages 253–266, 1994.

[88] A J Gonzalez and D D Dankel. *The Engineering of Knowledge-Based Systems: Theory and Practice*. Prentice Hall, 1993.

[89] W E L Grimson. *Object Recognition By Computer: The Role of Geometric Constraints*. MIT Press, Cambridge, Mass., 1990.

[90] G D Hager. The x-vision system: A general purpose substrate for real-time vision-based robotics. In *Proc. Workshop on Vision For Robots*, pages 56–63, 1995.

[91] G D Hager. A modular system for robust positioning using feedback from stereo vision. *IEEE Trans. on Robotics and Automation*, 13(4), Aug. 1997.

[92] G D Hager and P N Belhumer. Efficient region tracking with parametric models of geometry and illumination. *IEEE Trans. on Pattern Analysis and Machine Intelligence*, 20(10):1025–1039, Oct. 1998.

[93] G D Hager and S Hutchinson. Introduction to the special section on vision-based control of robot manipulators. *IEEE Trans. on Robotics and Automation*, 12(5), Oct. 1996.

[94] T Hague, J A Marchant, and N D Tillet. Autonomous robot navigation for precision horticulture. In *IEEE Int. Conf. on Robotics and Automation*, pages 1880–5, April 1997.

[95] E S Haldane. *The Philosophical Works of Descartes*, volume 1. Cambridge University Press, London, 1911.

[96] S K Halgamuge and M Glesner. Neural networks in designing fuzzy systems for real world applications. *International Journal for Fuzzy Sets and Systems*, 65(1):1–12, 1994.

[97] R M Haralick and L G Shapiro. *Computer and Robot Vision*, volume 1. Addison-Wesley Publishing Company, Reading, MA, 1993.

[98] R M Haralick and L G Shapiro. *Computer and Robot Vision*, volume 2. Addison-Wesley Publishing Company, Reading, MA, 1993.

[99] D Harwood, M Subbarao, H Hakalahti, and L S Davis. A new class of edge-preserving smoothing filters. *Pattern Recognition Letters*, 6(3):155–162, 1987.

[100] L Henriksen, O Ravn, and N A Andersen. Autonomous vehicle interaction with indoor environments. In *5th International Symposium on Experimental Robotics*, New Jersey, USA, 1997. IEEE.

[101] D A Holton and J W Lloyd. *Algebra and Gemetry*. Charles Babbage Research Centre:Manitoba, Canada, 1978.

[102] A Hormann and U Rembold. Development of an advanced robot for autonomous assembly. In *IEEE Int. Conf. on Robotics and Automation*, pages 2452–7, 1991.

[103] B K P Horn. Obtaining shape from shading information. In P H Winston, editor, *The Psychology of Computer Vision*, pages 115–155. McGraw-Hill Book Company, New York, NY, 1975.

[104] B K P Horn. *Robot vision*. MIT Press, Cambridge, Mass., 1986.

[105] B K P Horn. Height and gradient from shading. *International Journal of Computer Vision*, 5(1):37–55, 1990.

[106] B K P Horn and M J Brooks. *Shape from Shading*. The MIT Press:Cambridge, Massachusetts:London, England, 1989.

[107] B K P Horn and R W Sjoberg. Calculating the reflectance map. *Applied Optics*, 18(11):1770–1779, 1979.

[108] I Horswill. Visual collision avoidance by segmentation. In *IROS '94. Proceedings of the IEEE/RSJ/GI International Conference on Intelligent Robots and Systems. Advanced Robotic Systems and the Real World*, pages 902–909, 1994.

[109] I D Horswill and R A Brooks. Situated vision in a dynamic world: Chasing objects. In *AAAI 88. Seventh National Conference on Artificial Intelligence.*, pages 796–800, 1988.

[110] A Howard and L Kitchen. Navigation using natural landmarks. *Robotics and Automous Systems*, 26:99–115, 1999.

[111] Andrew Howard and Les Kitchen. Navigation without localisation: a reactive network approach. In *Proceedings of the Fourth International Conference on Control, Automation, Robotics, and Vision*, pages 873–877, 1996.

[112] Andrew Howard and Les Kitchen. Fast visual mapping for mobile robot navigation. In *ICIPS '97 - IEEE Int. Conf. on Intelligent Signal Processing*, Proceedings of the 1997 IEEE International Conference on Intelligent Processing Systems, pages 1251–1255, New Jersey, USA, Oct. 1997. IEEE.

[113] S Hutchinson, G D Hager, and P I Corke. A tutorial on visual servo control. *IEEE Trans. on Robotics and Automation*, 12(5):651–670, Oct. 1996.

[114] R V Ifremer-Irisa and M L Lib-Ubo. Absolute location of underwater vehicles by acoustic data fusion. In *Proceedings of the IEEE Int. Conf. on Robotics and Automation*, pages 1310–1315, 1990.

[115] K Ikeuchi and B K P Horn. Numerical shape from shading and occluding boundaries. *Artificial Intelligence*, 17(1-3):114–184, Aug. 1981.

[116] S S Iyengar, C C Jorgesen, S V N Rao, and C R Weisbin. Robot navigation algorithms using learned spatial graphs. *Robotica*, 4(2):93–100, April-June 1986.

[117] D J Fleet J L Barron and S S Beauchemin. Performance of optical flow techniques. *International Journal of Computer Vision*, 12(1):43–77, 1994.

[118] F Janabi-Sharifi and W J Wilson. Automatic selection of image features for visual servoing. *IEEE Trans. on Robotics and Automation*, 13(6):890–903, Dec. 1997.

[119] R Jarvis. A sensor driven autonomous mobile robot: The whole system. In *Proceedings of the 6th Australian Joint Conference on Artificial Intelligence.AI'93.*, pages 423–31, 93.

[120] R A Jarvis. Collision-free trajectory planning using distance transforms. *Transactions of the Institution of Engineers, Australia, Mechanical Engineering*, ME10(3):187–91, Sept. 1985.

[121] X. Y. Jiang and H. Bunke. Vision planner for an intelligent multisensory vision system. Technical Report IAM-93-017, Institut für Informatik, Universität Bern, Schweiz, September 1993.

[122] T Jochem, D Pomerleau, and C Thorpe. Vision guided lane transition. In *1995 IEEE Symposium on Intelligent Vehicles*, pages 30–5, 1995.

[123] M Johnson. *The Body in the Mind*. University of Chicago Press, Chicago, 1987.

[124] D M McKeown Jr, W A Harvey Jr, and J McDermott. Rule-based interpretation of aerial imagery. *IEEE Trans. on Pattern Analysis and Machine Intelligence*, PAMI-7(5):570–585, Sept. 1985.

[125] P Kahn, L Kitchen, and E M Riseman. A fast line finder for vision-guided robot navigation. *IEEE Trans. on Pattern Analysis and Machine Intelligence*, 12(11):1098–1102, November 1990.

[126] I Kant. *Critique of Pure Reason*. Orion Publishing Group:London, England, 1994.

[127] D Kappey, J Raczkowsky, U Rembold, and R Dillmann. Knowledge-based object recognition with uncertainty handling mechanisms. In *Proceedings of an International Conference. Intelligent Autonomous Systems 2. IOS*, volume 1, pages 393–9, 1990.

[128] O Khatib. Real-time obstacle avoidance for manipulators and mobile robots. *International Journal of Robotics Reasearch*, 5(1):396–404, 1986.

[129] K Kluge and C. E. Thorpe. Explicit models for robot road following. *IEEE Int. Conf. on Robotics and Automation*, pages 1148–1154, 1989.

[130] J J Koenderink and A J van Doorn. The internal representation of solid shape with respect to vision. *Biological Cybernetics*, 32(4):211–216, 1979.

[131] H Kollnig and H Nagel. 3d pose estimation by directly matching polyhdral models to gray value gradients. *International Journal of Computer Vision*, 23(3):283–302, 1997.

[132] B Kosko. *Fuzzy Engineering*. Prentice-Hall, New Jersey, 1997.

[133] E Krotov, M Herbert, and R Simmons. Stereo perception and dead reckoning for a prototype lunar rover. *Autonomous Robots*, 2(4):313–331, 1995.

[134] C-H Ku and W-H Tsai. Obstacle avoidance for autonomous land vehicle navigation in indoor environments by quadratic classifier. *IEEE Trans. on Systems, Man, and Cybernetics*, 29(3):416–426, June 1999.

[135] B J Kuipers and Y-T Byun. A robust qualitative approach to a spatial learning mobile robot. In *SPIE Vol. 1003 Sensor Fusion: Spatial Reasoning and Scene Interpretation*, pages 366–75, 1988.

[136] K N Kutulakos and C R Dyer. Recovering shape by purposive viewpoint adjustment. *International Journal of Computer Vision*, 12(2-3):113–126, 1994.

[137] G Lakoff. *Women, Fire, and Dangerous Things*. University of Chicago Press:Chicago, 1990.

[138] M Lamboley, C Proy, L Rastel, T N Trong, A Zashchirinski, and S Buslaiev. Marsokhod: Autonomous navigation tests on a mars-like terrain. *Autonomous Robots*, 2(4):345–351, 1995.

[139] X Lebegue and J K Aggarwal. Significant line segments for an indoor mobile robot. *IEEE Trans. on Robotics and Automation*, 9(6):801–15, Dec. 1993.

[140] C-H Lee and A Rosenfeld. Albedo estimation for scene segmentation. *Pattern Recognition Letters*, 1(3):155–160, 1983.

[141] C H Lee and A Rosenfeld. Improved methods of estimating shape from shading using the light source coordinate system. *Artificial Intelligence*, 26(2):125–143, May 1985.

[142] D Lee. A provably convergent algorithm for shape from shading. In B K P Horn and M J Brooks, editors, *Shape From Shading*, pages 349–373. The MIT Press: Cambridge Massachusetts, London England, 1989.

[143] J L Leonard and H F Durrant-Whyte. Mobile robot localizations by tracking geometric beacons. *IEEE Trans. on Robotics and Automation*, 7(3):376–382, June 1991.

[144] T C Leuth, U M Nassal, and U Rembold. Reliability and integrated capabilities of locomotion and manipulation for autonomous robot assembly. *Robotics and Automous Systems*, 14:185–198, 1995.

[145] S Linnainmaa, D Harwood, and L S Davis. Pose determination of a three-dimensional object using triangle pairs. *IEEE Trans. on Pattern Analysis and Machine Intelligence*, 10(5):634–647, Sept. 1988.

[146] D G Lowe. Three-dimensional object recognition from single two-dimensional images. *Artificial Intelligence*, 31(3):355–395, 1987.

[147] T Lozano-Perez. Automatic planning of manipulator transfer movements. *IEEE Trans. on Systems, Man, and Cybernetics*, SMC-11(10):681–698, Oct. 1981.

[148] T Lozano-Perez. Spatial planning: A configuration space approach. *IEEE Trans. on Computers*, C-32(2):108–120, Feb. 1983.

[149] Y Lu and R C Jain. Reasoning about edges in scale space. *IEEE Trans. on Pattern Analysis and Machine Intelligence*, 14(4):450–467, Apr. 1992.

[150] T C Lueth, U M Nassal, and U Rembold. Reliability and integrated capabilities of locomotion and manipulation for autonomous robot assembly. *Robotics and Automous Systems*, 14(2-3):185–198, May 1997.

[151] P Maes and R A Brooks. Learning to coordinate behaviours. In *AAAI 88. Seventh National Conference on Artificial Intelligence.*, pages 796–802, 1990.

[152] J Malik and D Maydan. Recovering three-dimensional shape from a single image of curved objects. *IEEE Transactions on Pattern Analysis and Machine*, 11(6):555–566, 1989.

[153] E H Mamdani. Application of fuzzy logic to approximate reasoning using linguistic synthesis. *IEEE Transactions on Computers*, 26(12):1182–1191, 1977.

[154] K Mandel and N A Duffie. On-line compensation of mobile robot docking errors. *IEEE Int. Journal of Robotics and Automation*, RA-3(6):591–598, Dec. 1987.

[155] D Marr. *Vision : a computational investigation into the human representation and processing of visual information.* W.H. Freeman, NY, 1982.

[156] J Marti, J Batlle, and A Casals. Model-based object recognition in industrial environments for autonomous vehicles control. In *IEEE Int. Conf. on Robotics and Automation*, pages 1632–7, April 1997.

[157] T Matsuyama. Expert systems for image processing: Knowledge-based composition of image analysis processes. *Computer Vision, Graphics, and Image Processing*, 48(1):22–49, 1989.

[158] L Matthies, E Gat, R Harrison, B Wilcox, R Volpe, and T Litwin. Mars microrover navigation: Performance evaluation and enhancement. In *IROS '95. Proceedings of the IEEE/RSJ International Conference on Intelligent Robots and Systems*, pages 433–40, August 1995.

[159] H B Meieran. Robotic and teleoperation activities at the chernobyl atomic power station: performance successes and limitations. In *Teleoperation and control 1988.Proceedings of the International Symposium.*, pages 25–31, 1988.

[160] M Minsky. A framework for representing knowledge. In Patrick H. Winston, editor, *The psychology of computer vision*, pages 211–277. McGraw-Hill, New York, 1975.

[161] A Mittal, A Valilaya, S Banerjee, and M Balakrishnan. Real time vision system for collision detection. *Computer Science and Infomatics*, 25(1):13–29, March 1995.

[162] R R Murphy and R C Arkin. Adaptive tracking for a mobile robot. In *Proc. 5th In. Symp. on Intelligent Control*, pages 1044–1049, Philadephia, PA, 1990.

[163] S K Nayar, K Ikeuchi, and T Kanade. Surface reflection: Physical and geometrical perspectives. *IEEE Trans. on Pattern Analysis and Machine Intelligence*, 13(7):611–634, 1991.

[164] A M Nazif and M D Levine. Low level image segmentation: An expert system. *IEEE Trans. on Pattern Analysis and Machine Intelligence*, PAMI-6(5):555–577, Sept. 1984.

[165] W L Nelson and I Cox. Local path control for an autonomous vehicle. In I J Cox and G T Wilfong, editors, *Autonomous Robot Vehicals*, pages 38–44. Springer-Verlag: New York, 1990.

[166] H T Nguyen and M Sugeno. *Fuzzy systems : modeling and control*. Kluwer Academic Publishers, Boston, 1998.

[167] F E Nicodemus, J C Richmond, J J Hsia, I W Ginsberg, and T Liperis. *Geometrical Considerations and Nomenclature for Reflectance*. NBS Monograph 160, National Bureau of Standards, U. S. Department of Commerce, Washington, D. C., Oct. 1977.

[168] J D Nicoud and P Machler. Robots for anti-personnel mine search. In *Intelligent Autonomous Vehicles 1995*, pages 289–93, 1995.

[169] N J Nilsson. A mobile automaton: An application of artificial intelligence techniques. In *Proc. of Int. Joint Conf. on Artificial Intelligence*, pages 56–61, 1969.

[170] J Oliensis. Shape from shading as a partially well-constructed problem. *Computer Vision, Graphics, and Image Processing*, 54(2):163–183, 1991.

[171] J Oliensis and P Dupuis. A global algorithm for shape from shading. In *Proc. Fourth Int. Conf. on Computer Vision*, pages 692–701, 1993.

[172] D Pagac, E M Nebot, and H Durrant-Whyte. An evidential approach to map-building for autonomous vehicles. *IEEE Trans. Robotics and Automation*, 14(4):623–629, August 1998.

[173] J Pages, J Aranda, and A Casals. A 3d vision system to model industrial environments for agv's control. In *Proceedings of the 24th International Symposium on Industrial Robots*, pages 701–708, 1993.

[174] K Pahlavan, T Uhlin, and J-O Eklundh. Active vision as a methodology. In *Active Perception*, pages 19–46. Lawrance Erlbaum Assoc., Hillsdale, NJ, 1993.

[175] R Palm. *Fuzzy systems : modeling and control*, chapter Design of Fuzzy Controllers, pages 227–272. Kluwer Academic Publishers, Boston, 1998.

[176] A Pentland. Local shading analysis. *IEEE Transactions on Pattern Analysis and Machine*, 6(2):41–50, 1984.

[177] A P Pentland. Finding the illuminant direction. *Journal of the Optical Society of America*, 72(4), 1982.

[178] A P Pentland. Linear shape from shading. *International Journal of Computer Vision*, 4(2):153–162, 1990.

[179] S Petitjean, J Ponce, and D J Kriegman. Computing exact aspect graphs of curved objects: Algebraic surfaces. *International Journal of Computer Vision*, 9(3):231–255, 1992.

[180] A Piegat. *Fuzzy Modeling and Control*. Physica-Verlag, New York, 2001.

[181] D Pomerleau. Neural network based autonomous navigation. In *Vision and Navigation*, pages 83–92. Klewer Academic Publishers, 1990.

[182] D Pomerleau. Ralph:rapidly adapting lateral position handler. In *1995 IEEE Symposium on Intelligent Vehicles*, pages 506–11, 1995.

[183] W H Press, B P Flannery, S A Teukolsky, and W T Vetterling. *Numerical Recipes in C The Art of Scientific Computing*. Cambridge, 1990.

[184] P Questa and G Sandini. Time to contact computation with a space-variant retina-line c-mos sensor. In *Proceedings of the International Conference on Intelligent Robots and Systems*, Osaka, Japan, 1996.

[185] D Raviv and M Herman. A unified approach to camera fixation and vision based road following. *IEEE Trans. on Systems, Man and Cybernetics*, 24(8):1125–1141, Aug. 1994.

[186] U Rembold. The karlsruhe autonomous mobile assembly robot. In *Proceedings of the IEEE Int. Conf. on Robotics and Automation*, pages 598–603, 1988.

[187] A A G Requicha. Representation of rigid solids: Theory, methods, and systems. *Computing Surveys*, 12(4):437–464, Dec. 1980.

[188] A A G Requicha and H B Voelcker. Constructive solid geometry. Technical Report Tech. Memo 25, Production Automation Project, Univ. Rochester, Rochester, NJ., Nov. 1977.

[189] L G Roberts. Machine perception of three-dimensional solids. In *Optical and Electro-Optical Information Processing*, pages 159–197. MIT Press, Cambridge, MA, 1965.

[190] A Rosenfeld and A C Kak. *Digital Picture Processing*, volume 1. Academic Press, Inc.,Orlando:Florida, 1982.

[191] A Rosenfeld and A C Kak. *Digital Picture Processing*, volume 2. Academic Press, Inc.,Orlando:Florida, 1982.

[192] G Sandini, F Gandolfo, E Grosso, and M Tistarelli. Vision during action. In *Active Perception*, pages 151–190. Lawrance Erlbaum Assoc., Hillsdale, NJ, 1993.

[193] J Santos-Victor and G Sandini. Uncalibrated obstacle detection using normal flow. *Machine Vision and Applications*, 9(3):130–137, 1996.

[194] J Santos-Victor and G Sandini. Embedded visual behaviours for navigation. *Robotics and Automous Systems*, 19(3-4):299–313, March 1997.

[195] J Santos-Victor and G Sandini. Visual behaviours for docking. *Computer Vision and Image Understanding*, 67(3):223–38, Sept. 1997.

[196] R Sargent, B Bailey, C Witty, and A Wright. Dynamic object capture using fast vision tracking. *A. I. Magazine*, 18(1):65–72, 1997.

[197] R C Schank and R P Abelson. *Scripts, Plans, Goals and Understanding*. Lawrence Erlbaum Associates, Hillsdale, N.J., 1977.

[198] H Schultz. Retrieving shape information from multiple images of a specular surface. *IEEE Trans. on Pattern Analysis and Machine Intelligence*, 16(2):195–201, 1994.

[199] J T Schwartz and M Sharir. A survey of motion planning and related geometric algorithms. *Artificial Intelligence Journal*, 37:157–169, 1988.

[200] J R Searle. *The rediscovery of the mind*. MIT Press, Cambridge, Mass., 1992.

[201] M Shelley. *Three Gothic Novels*, chapter Frankenstien, pages 257–497. Penguin, 1986.

[202] Y Shirai. *Three-dimensional computer vision: Yoshiaki Shirai*. Berlin: New York: Springer-Verlag, 1987.

[203] M Simaan. Knowledge-guided segmentation of texture images. *IEEE Int. Conf. on Systems Engineering*, pages 539–542, 1990.

[204] R Simmons and S Koenig. Probabilistic navigation in partially observable environments. In *IJCAI'95*, pages 1080–1087, Montreal, Quebec, August 1995.

[205] H A Simon. *The Sciences of the Artificial*. MIT Press, Cambridge, Mass., 1969.

[206] M V Srinivasan, J S Chahl, M G Nagle, K Weber, S Venkatesh, and S W Zhang. *Computational Intelligence: A Dynamic System Perspective*, chapter Low-Level Vision in Insects, and Applications to Robot Navigation, pages 312–326. IEEE Press, 1995.

[207] M V Srinivasan, M Lehrer, W Kirchner, and S W Zhang. Range perception through apparent image speed in free-flying honeybees. *Visual Neuroscience*, 6:519–535, 1991.

[208] M E Stieber, C P Trudel, and D G Hunter. Robotic systems for the international space station. In *IEEE Int. Conf. on Robotics and Automation*, pages 3068–3073, April 1997.

[209] M Sugeno and G T Kang. Structure identification of fuzzy model. *Fuzzy Sets and Systems*, 28:15–33, Feb. 1988.

[210] K Sugihara. *Machine Interpretation of Line Drawings*, chapter 10. MIT Press, Cambridge, MA, 1986.

[211] S Sull and B Sridhar. Runway obstacle detection by controlled spatiotemporal image flow disparity. *IEEE Trans. on Robotics and Automation*, 15(3):537–547, June 1999.

[212] K T Sutherland and W B Thompson. Localizing in unstructured environments: Dealing with errors. *IEEE Trans. on Robotics and Automation*, 10(6):740–754, December 1994.

[213] T Takagi and M Sugeno. Fuzzy identification of systems and its applications to modelling and control. *IEEE Trans. on Systems, Man, and Cybernetics*, SMC-15(1):116–132, Feb. 1985.

[214] R Talluri and J K Aggarwal. Position estimation for an autonomous mobile robot in an outdoor environment. *IEEE Trans. on Robotics and Automation*, 8(5):573–584, Oct. 1992.

[215] R Talluri and J K Aggarwal. Mobile robot self-localisation using model-image feature correspondence. *IEEE Trans. on Robotics and Automation*, 12(1):63–77, Feb. 1996.

[216] K Tanaka, T Ikeda, and H O Wang. Fuzzy regulators and fuzzy observers: relaxed stability conditions and lmi-based design. *IEEE Transactions on Fuzzy Systems*, 6(2):250–265, May 1998.

[217] T Tanaka and M Sugeno. *Fuzzy systems : modeling and control*, chapter Introduction to fuzzy modelling, pages 61–89. Kluwer Academic Publishers, Boston, 1998.

[218] A M Thompson. The navigation system of the jpl robot. In *Proc. of Int. Joint Conf. on Artificial Intelligence*, pages 749–757, 1977.

[219] C Thorpe, M H Herbert, T Kanade, and S A Shafer. Vision and navigation for the carnegie-mellon navlab. *IEEE Trans. on*

Pattern Analysis and Machine Intelligence, 10(3):451–465, May 1988.

[220] S Thrun. To know or not to know: On the utility of models in mobile robotics. *A. I. Magazine*, 18(1):47–54, 1997.

[221] S Thrun. Learning metric-topological maps for indoor mobile robot navigation. *Artificial Intelligence*, 99(1):21–71, Feb. 1998.

[222] M Tistarelli and G Sandini. On the advantages of polar and log-polar mapping for direct estimation of time-to-impact from optical flow. *IEEE Trans. on Pattern Analysis and Machine Intelligence*, 15(4):401–410, April 1993.

[223] P-S Tsai and M Shah. Shape from shading using linear approximation. *Image and Vision Computing*, 12(8):487–498, Oct 1994.

[224] Roger Y. Tsai. A versatile camera calibration technique for high-accuracy 3D machine vision metrology using off-the-shelf TV cameras and lens. *IEEE Journal of Robotics and Automation*, RA-3(4):323–344, August 1987.

[225] T Tsubouchi and S Yuta. Matching between an abstracted real image and a generated image from environment map for the map assisted mobile robot's vision system. In *Robots: Coming of Age. Proceedings of the International Symposium and Exposition on Robots. Designated the 19th ISIR by the International Federation of Robotics.*, pages 338–351, 1988.

[226] V Tucakov and D G Lowe. Temporally coherent stereo: Improving performance through knowledge of motion. In *IEEE Int. Conf. on Robotics and Automation*, pages 1999–2006, April 1997.

[227] S Ullman and R Basri. Recognition by linear combinations of models. *IEEE Trans. on Pattern Analysis and Machine Intelligence*, 13(10):992–1006, October 1991.

[228] S Uras, F Girosi, A Verri, and V Torre. A computational approach to motion perception. *Biological Cybernetics*, 60:79–87, 1988.

[229] D L Vaughn and R C Arkin. Workstation recognition using a constrained edge-based hough transform for mobile robot nav-

igation. In *Proceedings SPIE:Sensor Fusion III:3D Perception and Recognition*, pages 503–514, 1990.

[230] W G Walter. *The Living Brain*. Penguin Books, Harmondsworth, Middlesex, UK., 1961.

[231] R Wang and H Freeman. Object recognition based on characteristic view classes. In *10th International Conference on Pattern Recognition, Atlantic City, NJ*, pages 8–12, 1990.

[232] W Wang and G G Grinstein. A survey of 3d solid reconstruction from 2d projection line drawings. *Computer Graphics Forum*, 12(2):137–158, 1993.

[233] N A Watts. Calculating the principle views of a polyhedron. In *9th International Conference on Pattern Recognition*, pages 316–322, 1988.

[234] O Wijk and H I Christensen. Triangulation-based fusion of sonar data with application in robot pose tracking. *IEEE Trans. Robotics and Automation*, 16(6):740–752, Dec. 2000.

[235] B H Wilcox and D B Gennery. A mars rover for the 1990's. In I J Cox and G T Wilfong, editors, *Autonomous Robot Vehicals*, pages 444–449. Springer-Verlag: New York, 1990.

[236] B H Wilcox, D B Gennery, A H Mishkin, B K Cooper, T B Lawton, N K Lay, and S P Katzmann. A vision system for a mars rover. In *Proceedings SPIE:Mobile Robots II*, pages 172–179, 1987.

[237] T Winograd. Three responses to situation theory. Technical Report CSLI-87-106, Center for the Study of Language and Information, Stanford University, Ventura Hall, Stanford, CA, 94305, 1987.

[238] L Wittgenstein. *Philosophical Investigations*. Blackwell:Oxford UK, 1996.

[239] M Xie. Matching free stereovision for detecting obstacles on a ground plane. *Machine Vision and Applications*, 9(1):9–13, 1996.

[240] E Yeh and D J Kriegman. Toward selecting and recognizing natural landmarks. In *IROS '94. Proceedings of the IEEE/RSJ International Conference on Intelligent Robots and Systems*, pages 47–53, August 1995.

[241] Z Zhang and O Faugeras. *3D Dynamic Scene Analysis*. Springer-Verlag, Berlin: Heidelberg: New York, 1992.

[242] Z Zhang, R Weiss, and A R Hanson. Obstacle detection based on qualitative and qantitative 3d reconstruction. *IEEE Trans. on Pattern Analysis and Machine Intelligence*, 19(1):15–26, Jan. 1997.

[243] Q Zheng and R Chellappa. Estimation of illuminant direction, albedo, and shape from shading. *IEEE Trans. on Pattern Analysis and Machine Intelligence*, 13(7):680–702, July 1991.

[244] T Zielke, M Braukmann, and W von Seelen. Cartrack: Computer vision-based car following. In *Proc. of the First IEEE Workshop on Applications of Computer Vision*, pages 156–163, 1992.

Index

Druck: Strauss Offsetdruck, Mörlenbach
Verarbeitung: Schäffer, Grünstadt